IN SEARCH OF LEGALITY
MIKHAIL M. SPERANSKII AND THE CODIFICATION OF RUSSIAN LAW

By
WILLIAM BENTON WHISENHUNT

EAST EUROPEAN MONOGRAPHS, BOULDER
DISTRIBUTED BY COLUMBIA UNIVERSITY PRESS, NEW YORK

2001

EAST EUROPEAN MONOGRAPHS, NO. DLXX

To my family

CONTENTS

ABBREVIATIONS

AAN   Arkhiv Akademii Nauk, St. Petersburg

MERSH   Wieczynski, Joseph L. ed. *Modern Encyclopedia of Russian and Soviet History*, 58 vols. Gulf Breeze, FL: Academic International Press, 1976-1992.

PSZ   *Polnoe Sobranie Zakonov Rossiiskoi Imperii*, 1st Ser., 45 vols. St. Petersburg, 1830.

RGIA   Rossiiskii Gosudarstvennii Istoricheskii Arkhiv, St. Petersburg

RNB   Rossiiskaia Natsionalnaia Biblioteka, otdel rukopisei, St. Petersburg

Second Section   Vtoroe otdelenie sobstvennoi Ego Imperatorskago Velichestva Kantseliarii (Second Section of His Imperial Majesty's Personal Chancery)

SZ   *Svod Zakonov Rossiiskoi Imperii*, 15 vols. St. Petersburg, 1833.

INTRODUCTION

This book examines one aspect of the long and productive career of one of Russia's most famous bureaucrats, Mikhail Mikhailovich Speranskii (1772-1839). Much of the historical literature on Speranskii focuses on his more liberal ideas of his early career under Alexander I. This is a study of his later career when he directed the efforts to codify Russian law. The codification of Russian law was perhaps his greatest achievement, yet it has received the least attention from scholars.

Two works were particularly influential during the conception of this work and as it progressed from a dissertation to a monograph. The classic biography of Speranskii by Marc Raeff[1] provided much of the general biographical information, references to valuable sources, and the inspiration for this project. Raeff notes in the beginning of his short chapter on codification in his biography that this subject has been neglected and should be studied. I hope this work begins to fill this gap in Speranskii's biography.

The other work is the outstanding work on legal consciousness in Russia up to the Great Reforms of the 1860s by Richard C. Wortman.[2] He focuses on the backgrounds, educational levels, service records and other factors of those men who reformed the Russia legal system in the 1860s. From Wortman's work, I began to ask the question about what exactly was being reformed. Hence, an analysis of the purpose and compilation of these two law codes from the 1830s seemed to be an appropriate project.

It is upon the basis of these two works that I organized this book. Chapter one examines Speranskii's background. While this is a subject well covered in other works, I link the progression of his career with his thoughts and writings on law. It is clear that his early personal writing was more liberal than his later plans for codification. Interestingly, these early ideas were even more liberal than many of those expressed in his early reform plans under Alexander I. Chapter two looks at the many attempts to codify Russian law since Peter the Great. Speranskii directed the work of the eleventh commission since 1700 called for the purpose of codifying Russian law. It is clear that, for more than a century, similar problems of imperial interference, confusion over Russian legality, and poorly trained assistants plagued each of the commissions. It was only during the reign of Alexander I that real progress was made in which Speranskii played a limited, yet important role.

Chapter three addresses the motivation behind or the purpose of the compilation of each law code. Speranskii certainly had his own ideas for a sense of legality. Clearly, Nicholas I had his as well. The result was the following of Nicholas' desires which did not completely satisfy Speranskii. In the third chapter as well, I examine in a more fundamental way how the work was organized, who did it, and how it was completed. This may appear a bit mundane, but much of the scope of the project was determined by how the work was organized. The last chapter looks at the foreign influences on how the laws of the Russian Empire were compiled. The clearest example in both codes of borrowing legal principles from abroad was in inheritance law. Foreign influence also presented itself as many of the assistants in the group were sent abroad for legal training. When they returned they brought many European ideas into this commission that were not necessarily consistent with Russian norms. More importantly, though, these students in the 1820s and 1830s who helped create a legal profession in Russia and the foundation for the legal reform of the 1860s. In the end, Speranskii's role and influence were clear. He personally collected laws, drafted sections of both codes, oversaw personnel, and traveled to investigate regional depositories. His last major bureaucratic undertaking before his death in 1839 was one his most significant of his long career.

As stated earlier, this book started as a doctoral dissertation in history at the University of Illinois at Chicago. A first note of thanks must go to my advisor, James Cracraft, for his help while in the program and since. I would also like to express a special thanks to Professor Ted Hinckley for reading this manuscript and offering valuable editorial advice. Steven A. Uusitalo and Alexander M. Martin also read parts of this work in a different form and were helpful for organization and clarity. Without a doubt, though, I must express my appreciation to my family for their support. My mother and father both poured over this manuscript more than once. Their extraordinary support of my work is of profound personal and professional importance to me. My wife, Michele, and my children, Meredith and Matthew, have tolerated the up and down nature of this kind of project. I thank them so much for their patience. Thanks to all of you for your help.

William Benton Whisenhunt
St. Charles, IL
November, 2000

NOTES

[1] Marc Raeff, *Michael Speransky: Statesman of Imperial Russia, 1772-1839* (The Hague: Martinus Nijhoff, 1957).

[2] Richard C. Wortman, *The Development of a Russian Legal Consciousness* (Chicago: University of Chicago Press, 1976).

CHAPTER ONE

MIKHAIL M. SPERANSKII:
A BIOGRAPHICAL SKETCH,
1772-1826

Mikhail Mikhailovich Speranskii (1772-1826) was one of the most important statesmen of Imperial Russia. By the time he was called to codify Russian law in 1826, he already had a distinguished and controversial career in the Russian government. Speranskii's early life and career were key factors in how and why he embarked on his last major bureaucratic reform effort under Nicholas I. The details of his early life are difficult to assemble because of a fire in 1834 that destroyed nearly all of Speranskii's personal papers.[1] From early in his career, Speranskii wrote essays on a variety of subjects related to government, politics, and political philosophy. The development of his career in conjunction with his legal though helped take Speranskii to the height of power and send him into exile in the first quarter of the nineteenth century.

Speranskii was born on January 1, 1772, in the village of Cherkutino in the Vladimir province, the son of a parish priest who died when the boy was young. Speranskii's mother was a woman of exceptional emotional and spiritual strength and his grandmother was a deeply pious woman who helped shape her grandson's mystical religious beliefs.[2] Speranskii's father tutored his son at home before he attended the seminary at Vladimir at the age of twelve. Many seminaries sufferred during the reign of Catherine II in her efforts to secularize education in the 1770s and 1780s. It was only under her son, Paul, that ecclesiastical education received increased financial support from the government. Speranskii's relatives in Vladimir were able to support him during his studies at the seminary. Most students and even many of the professors lived in poor conditions and had to spend much of their time finding sources of income for survival rather than pursuing intellectual or spiritual matters.[3] Because of his family's financial support, Speranskii dedicated more time to his studies and often excelled in his courses. At times, he even substituted for his instructors. As a result of his superior academic work, Speranskii was chosen to attend the Aleksandr Nevskii Monastery in St. Petersburg. His best performance was in mathematics and philosophy. Upon graduation he was offered a faculty position, but he turned it down and entered the civil service.[4] In the late 1780s and early 1790s, as Speranskii went from student to instructor at the Aleksandr Nevskii Monastery, he began to formulate his own ideas on law. In the one of Speranskii's earliest essays, which he wrote before he was twenty years old, he invoked religious imagery and biblical scriptures to emphasis the importance of proper moral behavior for political leaders. Speranskii believed strongly that the proper foundation of government was a firm and clear set of laws that provided an "ethical and religious approach to political rule".[5]

By the mid-1790s, Speranskii launched an attack on the proper behavior of specific political leaders. At the end of Catherine II's reign, she turned away from many of her more liberal ideas concerning government because of the French Revolution. Speranskii expressed his disappointment with her conservative turn and the immoral behavior of many officials in her government. He wrote that

If by the most devious ways you [Catherine] *seize all the possessions of your subjects, if you let them feel the weight of your hand and convince them through fear that you are more than an* [ordinary] *human being: then, with all your talents, and the luster, you be but a fortunate criminal; the flatterers will enter your name in golden letters on the list of most outstanding intellects, but later history will add with a black blush that you were a tyrant of your country.*[6]

Marc Raeff concludes that Speranskii's attack was an unsophisticated indictment of the aging empress. Another biographer and protege of Speranskii's asserted that his mentor was simply making a general statement on the corrupt conditions among officials in the Russian administration.[7]

His talents were becoming well-known and were increasingly in demand. He was well-known for his diligent work ethic and his excellent performance as a student. In 1797, Speranskii took the position of personal secretary to Prince A.B. Kurakin, who served as Procurator General of the Senate for Paul. He moved quickly up the Table of Ranks and achieved hereditary noble status by the end of his career under Nicholas I. He impressed some of the most inept and brutal officials during Paul's reign. While serving Paul loyally in the late 1790s, he became better acquainted with the emperor's son, Alexander, and Alexander Radishchev. Catherine had exiled Radishchev in 1790 for his book, *A Journey from St. Petersburg to Moscow*, which illuminated the terrible living and working conditions of the Russian peasantry. Paul called Radishchev back to government service where he served on a commission on laws with Speranskii. The brief interaction between the two men had a positive intellectual impact on the latter.[8]

The St. Petersburg social scene provided additional avenues for advancement for civil servants. Upon his arrival in the capital, Speranskii became re-aquainted with a Russian Orthodox priest from his youth, Andrei A. Samborskii, who was a well-established cultural and religious leader in St. Petersburg. Samborskii had served as the chaplain for the Russian Embassy in London under Catherine II so he was very familiar with current English religious thought. He promoted English ideas on religion, philosophy, and other subjects in his home in St. Petersburg which had become an intellectual and social center at a time when terror and repression tainted French Enlightenment ideas.[9]

Speranskii's close aquaintance with Samborskii enabled him to move in the highest social circles in St. Petersburg. Even though Speranskii did not like these social situations, he made professional connections with many government officials who helped him move up the bureaucratic ranks. It was also through Samborskii that Speranskii met his future wife, Elizabeth Stephens. Initially, their only common language was French, but this did not impede their courtship.

They were married in 1798, and had a daughter the following year. However, Stephens never fully recovered from childbirth and died in 1800. Speranskii was deeply upset by the death of his wife and withdrew from many of his social engagements. His close personal friend and government official, V.N. Karazin helped Speranskii through this difficult personal period and brought Speranskii's bureaucratic talents to the attention of the new emperor, Alexander I. For much of the rest of his life, Speranskii remained aloof from St. Petersburg social life which created many enemies at the Russian court.[10]

The turn of the century brought two dramatic changes in Speranskii's life. First, his friend and colleague, Radishchev had grown tired of the work of the Legislative Commission. He promoted more abstract ideas about law while his colleagues, Speranskii included, were more interested in the bureaucratic demands. Radishchev had fallen into a depression about his work, his health, the strain for money and his continued loss of status in Russian society. In a fit, Radishchev drank nitric acid that his son had prepared for polishing. He died the next day.[11] Paul had initiated many changes in Russia during his short reign, but they were generally poorly planned or contradictory. For instance, Paul wanted to launch an attack on the French in 1798 for killing their monarch during the French Revolution, but just a year later agreed with Napoleon to send a regiment of Don Cossacks into India. Neither plan had a clear objective nor were they well executed. Most historians agree that the erratic and widely disliked Paul was kidnapped and eventually killed by Alexander's group of friends, some of whom later became members of his "Unofficial Committee". As Alexander took the throne, Speranskii began his most influential period in government service, from 1802 until 1812.[12]

Soon after Alexander I took the throne, Speranskii was transferred to the Section for Civilian and Ecclesiastical Affairs under the newly-founded Council of State. Despite his estrangement from St. Petersburg social circles, Speranskii's talents were in demand, and several ministries began to compete for his services. Count Victor Kochubei won the battle and had Speranskii transferred to the Second Department of the Ministry of the Interior in 1802, where he was in charge of police duties and remained in this position until 1807. In this position, Speranskii founded a newspaper, *St. Petersburg Journal (Sankt Peterburgskii Zhurnal)*, as an official organ of the government, and supported the issuance of annual reports in order to communicate more effectively with the Russian people. At this early stage of his career, Speranskii undertook the reform of the Ministry of Internal Affairs which became a model for many of his future reform projects.[13]

Ironically, the Interior Ministry had just been reorganized in 1801, but it was still riddled with problems. Speranskii organized most of this reform under the direction of Kochubei. In this reform, Speranskii recognized several inherent problems in the Russian administration which would help him carry out his later reforms of the entire ministerial system in 1810-1811. The work of the Interior Ministry was often frustrated by its slow pace which often created a backlog of more than a year. Speranskii attributed the slow work pace to here being no division of labor or real hierarchy within the ministry. Speranskii created divisions and more internal positions within the ministry to make it function more efficiently. He also altered the way each member of the ministry worked. Often each member would be bogged down with an excessively formal environment, especially the use of the formal correspondence for simple and routine tasks. Speranskii tried to make the internal communication more efficient. However, the most perplexing problem Speranskii faced as he reformed this ministry was the incompetent officials who received their position because of their status in Russian society, not their merit. [14]

Despite Speranskii's intense work schedule, he also took time to write more abstract essays on the nature of government and law. In 1802, Speranskii wrote "On Fundamental Laws of the State, (1802)," one of his first political works, which addressed the question of whether or not Russia could live under the rule of law without infringing on the power of the autocrat. Speranskii's service under Paul instilled in him a fear of tyrannical government. David Christian asserts that Speranskii believed a constitution had to come from the people of a nation, but most observers understood that the Russian people were not politically sophisticated enough for this to happen. Concern for daily survival preoccupied the Russian population, which was still more than eighty-percent enserfed.[15]

This document clearly was one of Speranskii's most radical proposals where he explicitly outlined how a constitution in Russia would need to limit the power of the autocracy. Speranskii claimed that early ninteenth-century Russia was not ready socially or politically for a constitution because the bulk of the Russian population had no voice nor avenue for real public expression before the emperor. The only way for a constitution to exist in Russia would be with the support of the population. Speranskii asserted that the people would need to "force" the autocrat to honor the constitution, the ultimate act of enforcement of a constitution, and as in the English example, would be a popular revolt.[16] Speranskii did not believe Russia was politically or socially ready for freedom. Christian summarizes Speranskii's argument as "the idea that a 'true monarchy' must be based on a definite social structure whose main feature was an enlightened, hereditary nobility, linked to the people by the institution of primogeniture".[17]

Speranskii claimed that autocracy and constitutionalism were incompatible concepts. He believed that a constitution must be derived from and created by the people and limitations placed upon the autocrat would destroy it and produce a "true monarchy," meaning one that resembled the English monarchy. According to one historian,

> *To Speranskij, 'constitution' meant the fundamental law of the Russian empire, and as such it was merely the working statement of the purpose and method followed by the Government in fulfilling its obligation of spiritual and moral leadership of the nation. And a primary condition for the viability it be founded on the true historical condition of Russia. And though Speranskij did use forms of organization introduced by Napoleon, though he did believe in a streamlined government apparatus and a separation of functions, he did not accept the basic premises of the atomistic, balance of power, social contract ideas of Western liberal and constitutional theories.[18]*

Speranskii further interpreted the ideas of Montesquieu on the nature of government as "From this it follows: 1) that fundamental laws of the state must be created by the people; 2) that the fundamental laws of the state place limits on the will of the autocrat".[19]

The historian must note that Montesquieu had identified three types of government in S*pirit of Laws* (1748). Montesquieu thought that a republic was only feasible in a small nation. Larger nations demanded a more centralized form of government. He and Speranskii agreed that England was the ideal form of monarchy, one that was restricted to a certain extent by law. As for despotism, Montesquieu believed that this was best reserved for large empires and maintained through fear. Montesquieu used early-eighteenth century Russia as an example of a nation trying to break free from despotic rule from the top down. He wrote:

> *Observe how the government of Moscow strives to emerge from despotism, which it finds more of a burden than does its people. It has suppressed its elite guards, made less severe punishments for crimes, established courts; it has even come to learn what laws are; and to provide instruction for its people.*[20]

Speranskii also called for the creation of a two-chambered assembly to consist of an upper house of nobles and a lower house of commoners (townspeople, merchants and peasants). While he was not explicit about whether this new body would be legislative or consultative, his overall intention to reform the Russian administration would tend to give more weight to the idea that this body was to be a legislative one. Speranskii believed strongly that a code of law and some measure of representation were essential in the fight against tyranny and chaos. However, Speranskii understood the traditional Russian institutions of autocracy and serfdom, and acknowledged that these realities would keep Russia from implementing a constitutional style government comparable to England. He asserted that social changes were necessary before massive political reforms could begin.[21] While this tract did not alter the Russian administration directly, Speranskii will use many ideas pronounced here for future reform plans.

Even though Kochubei often took credit for Speranskii's ideas, they both understood the importance of implementing reforms. Speranskii's idea for rationalizing government institutions were closely linked to the men who ran the agencies because a fully transformed bureaucracy required an enhancement of the quality of government officials. He wanted appointments to be based on preparation and merit (much as Peter the Great had designed in his Table of Ranks), instead of the traditional method of awarding positions to the nobility regardless of ability.[22]

Throughout Speranskii's career the issue of education repeatedly arose in several different ways. Alexander reorganized the entire educational system under the direction of two members of the "Unofficial Committee," Count Grigorii Stroganov and Prince Adam Czartoryski. Because of his experience as a seminary student, Speranskii was selected to direct the reforms of the seminaries which were still suffering great neglect that began under the new emperor's grandmother. It was here that Speranskii asked to implement small-scale reforms first in order to test their effectiveness before they were implemented empire-wide. Raeff notes that this proposed method was unusual because "until then, statutes had been issued for immediate execution, and any inconveniences revealed by experience were corrected – if at all – much too late".[23]

Speranskii realized early in his career that two basic problems plagued the entire Russian government. First, there was a widespread lack of funding for nearly every project or department of government, and secondly, nearly every department lack properly-trained bureaucrats. He took it upon himself to try to educate them on the nature of their work and on the way economic activity was linked to government activity in Russia. Even though his efforts for the most part were in vain, he continued to push for expansion of educational opportunities for government officials for the rest of his career.

In 1808, with the endorsement of Alexander I and help of I. Martynov of the Ministry of Education, Speranskii helped found a lyceum at Tsarskoe Selo to be under the direct control of the emperor and designed to train sons of the nobility for bureacratic careers. Formal legal education at the lyceum did not emerge until after Speranskii's time. There had been several efforts at establishing institutions for the teaching of law, but none were successful. Catherine attempted to train young noblemen in the Cadet Corps for careers in the bureaucracy. Earlier in Alexander's reign in 1804, he tried to establish a similar institution under the control of the Senate with the same results. However, not everyone in the Russian administration and court agreed with the creating of this school. Some of Speranskii's critics thought that he was infected with French ideas and that this lyceum was just a tool to promote his liberal ideals. For example, Joseph de Maistre, a Sardinian diplomat, through family connections to the Russian nobility and acceptance in the salons of St. Petersburg, strongly opposed Speranskii's enlightened and rational ideas, claiming that they would only subvert traditional Russian culture and the Russian autocracy.[24]

Later in 1808, Speranskii was transferred to the Ministry of Justice and assigned the weighty task of codifying Russian law by the emperor. This was the tenth codification commission since the era of Peter the Great. Alexander had inherited the ninth such commission from his father at the beginning of the century, but the failures of its elderly, inept, and reactionary director, P.A. Zavadovskii, and the suicide of one of its most prominent and productive members, Alexander Radishchev, had left the work incomplete.[25]

With these failures in mind, Alexander I demanded results from this commission. He wanted Speranskii to draw up a code of laws similar to what Napoleon had promulgated in 1800 *(Code Napoleon)*. Speranskii accepted the challenge but because he was not specifically educated in law and because of the disorganized and fragmentary nature of Russian law, he reorganized the commission and looked to other nations for legal models. France's new code appealed the most to Speranskii because of its democratic parts. Most observers, though, realized that "France was headed for a regime at least as autocratic as and even more centralized than that of Louis XIV".[26]

Speranskii hastily prepared a civil code,[27] commonly known as the "Plan of 1809," which drew heavily on the French *Code Napoleon*. This plan was drafted in secret for Alexander, but soon after he submitted it to the emperor, he was removed from his position as State Councillor. Speranskii's plan outlined how a country like Russia, one dominated by autocracy, could be transformed into one based on law. First, the autocracy needed to be limited by the rule of law. Beyond that, Speranskii advocated the creation of a system with three branches, each having separate functions. Speranskii drew heavily on

Montesquieu's *Spirit of Laws* and the new government in the United States as models for this idea. While in the American model, the sovereignty rests in all three branches, Speranskii gave sovereignty to only the executive branch or the emperor which left the other two branches, legislative and judicial, merely consultative. Speranskii expressly indicated when the legislative and judicial sections were allowed to take binding action without the consent of the executive power: "1) when a government measure clearly violates the basic law of the state, for example with regard to personal and political freedom; 2) when a government fails at the set time to submit the accounts required by law".[28] His plan did not specifically limit the power of the autocrat, but the structure and wording of the plan frightened Alexander and Russian conservatives. Speranskii also believed that different societies in the world developed at different paces socially, politically, and culturally toward a more modern order. For Russia it was developing at a difficult pace than in the United States, England, or France. One historian notes that

> *This approach,* [historicism] *argued in Russia by Karamzin, and formulated by* [Friedrich] *Savigny and the German historical school of jurisprudence, presented the laws of each nation as expressions of that nations particular characteristics and needs. It banished the notion that law had to conform to universal nature norms, and consecrating the statutes issued by the autocrat, exempted them from outside judgment. Codification then became the ordering and compilation of the ruler's legislative acts, the precondition to the precise implementation of his will.*[29]

Historiographical debates have erupted over the nature of Speranskii's plan. Raeff presents Speranskii as a loyal servant to the emperor not interested in tearing down the autocracy. Others, like John Gooding, present Speranskii as a shrewd bureaucrat who knew that he could not openly advocate the destruction of the autocracy in Russia, so instead engaged in self-censorship, but he was a true constitutionalist.[30] Either way, Speranskii ran afoul of the emperor and left himself politically vulnerable in 1810 and 1811.

This new framework did not appeal to Alexander as well. The majority of the Russian population was enserfed and uneducated, and, in general, the nobility resisted education. Clearly, this system of government required a large group of bureaucrats so educational reforms would also be needed. It was clear to Speranskii that Russia's social system made this political system nearly impossible in the near future. Speranskii strongly believed that Russia's educational levels had to be elevated before real social, legal, or political changes could take place. In support of this view, Speranskii wrote in 1809 that

The kingdoms of this world have their periods of rise and fall, and in every period the structure of government must be compatible with the educational level of the citizens upon which the state rests. Whenever the form of government falls below of rises above that level, the state will be shaken by greater or lesser convulsions. In general this is what explains the political upheavals which in ancient times and in our own days changed the course of governments. This also explains the failure which often accompany the most beneficent political reforms when public education had not adequately prepared men's minds.[31]

In the "Plan of 1809," Speranskii also addressed the issue of rights of Russian citizens. He used Catherine II's model of three distinct classes in Russian society: mobility, townspeople, and peasants. While Speranskii in other writings condemned serfdom, he did not take it into account in this plan, and failed to make clear distinctions between free peasants which left this proposal suspect. He expected all Russians to be accountable before the law and for the law to serve all Russians fairly according to class. Speranskii divided rights into civil and political categories and as expected, the nobility faired better. Despite his abhorrence of serfdom, he provided a provision in its defense when he asserted that "No one may be compelled to render services at someone's arbitrary command, but only on the basis of law defining the nature of service according to estates".[32]

The political rights were also heavily weighted in favor of the nobility in Speranskii's proposal. They were "1) common civil rights belonging to all subjects; 2) particular civil rights which ought to belong only to those who are prepared for them by their way of life and education; 3) political rights belonging to those who own property".[33] The last two provisions expressly excluded nearly all of the peasantry and most of the townspeople from holding any real political rights. Few common people had any education and were not prepared in their way of life, according to Speranskii's definition, for such rights. The third part clearly ensured that serfs and most peasants had no political rights because of the necessity of owning property.

These political rights, in Speranskii's plan, would be expressed in the duma. The duma had four levels. The township level handled issues of local fiscal and educational concern. The district level duma oversaw the activities of the numerous township dumas. From the district dumas, members of the provincial dumas were selected and likewise members of the State Duma were selected from the provincial level.[34]

The State Duma sat for one year and was responsible for organizing state laws, civil laws, statutes and regulations, ministerial accounts, needs of the state, and finances. All legislative initiatives were submitted to the State Duma by the heads of the ministries in the name of the emperor, with three exceptions. The State Duma could take unilateral action on issues of the "needs of the state" because these were purely bureaucratic matters, according to Speranskii. The State Duma had disciplinary powers on all branches of government, including the executive, for officials who failed to fulfill their responsibilities. The State Duma also reviewed laws passed by a lower duma that violated the laws of the state. On the surface, Speranskii's State Duma appeared to limit the power of the executive, but in reality Speranskii noted earlier that the autocrat had the power to stop the State Duma's work by "1) adjournment to the following year; [or] 2) dismissal of all members".[35]

The "Plan of 1809" showed a number of interesting legal ideas. It appeared to be a constitution that placed limits on the power of the autocracy; but when examined more closely, it included a defense of autocracy, nobility, and serfdom. It is important to note the distinction between different definitions of "constitution". Speranskii's plan was not a document along the lines of the French and American constitutional models of the eighteenth century, but it did outline powers (however limited) of the different branches of government that consisted of popularly elected (also limited) representatives which had never existed before in Russia. Speranskii exhibited his enthusiasm for European enlightened ideas in this document. He seemed most heavily influenced by Montesquieu's general concepts, but rejected many of the details in favor of Russian tradition.

Speranskii's timing could not have been worse as tensions were rising between Russia and Napoleon. Nikolai Karamzin, writer and official historian for Alexander I, criticized Speranskii openly for being a Francophile and for simply translating portions of the French code and imposing it blindly upon Russia. Karamzin exaggerated the French influence on Speranskii's work to promote his more conservative ideological position and to warn of the impending invasion by Napoleon.

By the middle of Alexander's reign, Russia's financial problems were tremendous, many of which were a legacy inherited from Catherine II's reign. She had given large gifts of state lands and serfs to many nobles, hence reducing state revenues. In the late eighteenth century and early ninteenth centuries, moreover, state expenditures far exceeded the revenue collected, and the war with Napoleon almost devastated Russia financially. Before Napoleon is invasion, Alexander assembled a group of bureaucrats familiar with the economy in Russia and abroad and drafted the "Financial Plan of 1810". Soviet historians attribute the work to jurist Mikhail A. Balug'ianskii (1769-1847), but L.H. Jacob, a Prussian economist and philosopher in service in Russia, took credit himself for the plan, but it was more likely that Balug'ianskii outlined the plan while Speranskii flushed out the more specific details. The main thrust of this plan was to raise revenue and decrease the deficit, but it alienated many nobles and created new enemies for Speranskii. The plan departed from Russian tradition by providing an all-encompassing theory on which the economy would be based and by borrowing foreign ideas concerning credit from the Scottish physiocrat Adam Smith. In the aftermath of the French Revolution, Speranskii's constant reliance on foreign legal ideas eventually contributed to his fall from power.[36]

Alexander issued the "Financial Plan of 1810"[37] in February of that year. In order to pay the debt completely Alexander commanded that no government agency could increase spending. To meet this goal, Speranskii advocated a twenty million ruble reduction in spending and an increase in taxes. Alexander did issue the original plan as it was submitted to him, but through this initial law and following minor laws, many of the ideas Speranskii and others on that commission supported were enacted as laws. By the summer of 1811, the reorganization of the Ministry of Finance was completed. Guided by Speranskii's plan, Alexander succeeded in raising state revenues and decreasing the debt; however, the toll on Russian society was great. The peasantry suffered a double tax for passports needed for internal travel. The nobility complained loudly because their wealth had been reduced because of the devaluing of the currency. By 1812, the Russian ruble had reached its lowest value in more than a century.[38]

The ministerial reform and the "Financial Plan of 1810" were two of Speranskii's greatest achievements, but Napoleon's invasion in 1812 disrupted them both. Russian war expenditures were so massive that the entire "Financial Plan of 1810" was abandoned, but Speranskii's efforts did make some impact. He helped stabilize the value of the ruble, introduced a rational system of fiscal administration, and brought Adam Smith's ideas of fiscal planning to Russia.[39]

Speranskii believed that reform of the central government was long overdue because of the chaotic nature of the central administration during the eighteenth century. Even after the ministerial reforms of the first years of Alexander's reign, the authority of each minister was still ambiguous and the responsibility for the administration of the country while the emperor was away was unclear. Speranskii identified three problems with the ministries: "insufficient responsibility of the individual ministers, lack of precision and proportion in the distribution of affairs among the ministries, and inadequate rules of procedure," all issues that plagued all of Speranskii's reform efforts.[40] By June 1811, Speranskii had finished the work of reorganizing the government, providing a structure which lasted until 1905. He restructured each ministry in the way work was conducted and in how the finances organized. Traditional Russian administration focused on security and raising money for the military with little regard for fiscal responsibility.

Speranskii's plan made the minister directly responsible for the ministry with a division of labor and responsibility within each ministry. Ministries were divided into departments headed by lower officials who reported to the minister. Hence lower officials made no policy reforms without the minister's consent, so they served merely in an advisory role.[41] Speranskii also expanded the role of private citizens in the ministries by calling together citizen groups to serve as consultants in certain areas where they could provide more expertise. This dramatic proposal, though, was not implemented until the 1830s and then only on a small scale.[42] The ministers were restricted from enacting legislation themselves, this was left to the emperor. Speranskii felt that with so many officials sending proposals to the emperor for review that it would be more efficient to create a council of ministers to summarize the most pressing legislative needs before the emperor.[43]

Earlier in 1811, the Council of State had been created to consider legislation and made recommendations to the emperor. The first council considered codification proposals from the Commission on Laws, the reorganization of the ministries, and Speranskii's "Plan of 1809" and "Financial Plan of 1810". The council remained as the supreme consultative body to the ruler throughout the nineteenth century and usually considered judicial and legal matters. Speranskii intended for it to be more like a parliament, according to his "Plan of 1809," but a consultative council was the best that could be accomplished at this point.[44]

Also by 1811, the forces that opposed Speranskii were growing. One of his first problems he had created for himself. Early in his career, especially after his wife's death, he had remained aloof from the social circles of St. Petersburg and generally only had contempt for this scene. He dedicated himself to his work and spent little time forging political alliances within the Russian administration and his perceived rejection of the political and social powers of St. Petersburg proved costly for him when he was attacked for his reform plans. Similarly, the old nobility of Moscow disliked Speranskii because of his humble origins and especially for his "Plan of 1809" which jeopardized the traditional role of thef nobility in Russian society.[45]

One of Speranskii's most serious problems was when he was implicated in a plot against Alexander in 1810-11, but how exactly this plot developed was unclear and evidently Speranskii had nothing to do with it. His enemies, especially his childhood friend, A.N. Golitsyn, suggested to the emperor that Speranskii was involved in this treasonous plot. A Swedish noble named Armfeldt and Minister of Police A. Balushev were supposedly allied with Speranskii in a plot to overthrow Alexander and rule through a triumvirate. Speranskii denied any involvement, but his coldness and sporadic involvement with mystics and Freemasons kept the emperor wondering whether one of his most important government officials was loyal to him or not. Speranskii's main opposition came from Joseph de Maistre who despised the philosophical and political ideas of the Enlightenment, and believed that Speranskii's espousal of these rational ideas was destroying traditional Russian society. De Maistre wanted Russia to maintain its traditional and religious foundations and not engage in the discussions that dominated Europe at this time regarding personal liberty and civil rights for all people. He identified the lyceum at Tsarskoe Selo as a breeding ground for this evil.[46]

De Maistre had established many close ties in Russian conservative intellectual circles, especially with S.S. Uvarov and Nikolai Karamzin who were part of the widespread anti-French revolutionary sentiment in Russia. Early in Alexander's reign, de Maistre had attended the traditional court of Dowager Empress Maria Fedorovna, a conservative group that especially opposed French enlightened thinking. However, after the diplomatic settlement at Tilsit in 1807, which allied Russia and French, de Maistre fell out of favor with the emperor, and Speranskii went on the enjoy his greatest influence.[47]

Speranskii's "Plan 1809" and the rising tensions with Napoleon provided de Maistre and other opponents with the opportunity to criticize his "liberal" ideas, especially his constitutional plans, which drew heavily on the French *Code Napoleon*. Specifically, de Maistre wrote an essay entitled *Essai sur le principe generateur des constitutions politiques* in late 1809 in response to Speranskii's constitutional plans. He attacked constitutionalism in general without addressing Speranskii directly, but the implications were clear enough. His criticisms found favor among his colleagues in his conservative circle and even with the emperor. Soon after de Maistre's *Essai* appeared, Karamzin submitted his *Memoir on Ancient and Modern Russia* (1811) to Alexander; its ideological argument coincided well with de Maistre's.[48]

Karamzin's *Memoir* was probably the best known example of intellectual opposition to Speranskii's plans; even though this document was not officially published until many years later, it circulated widely in manuscript form. Karamzin submitted it to Alexander in an effort to warn the emperor of the supposed dangers of Speranskii's proposals, especially that Speranskii's alleged constitutional plans would destroy the nobility and eventually the monarchy in Russia, the old-age bulwarks of the autocratic system.

More specifically, Karamzin attacked Speranskii's "Plan of 1809" on two points. First, he asserted that Speranskii's plan borrowed too heavily from the *Code Napoleon*. He posed this question:

Is it why have toiled for one thousand years or so to produce our own comprehensive code, in order now to confess solemnly to all Europe that we are all fools, and bow our gray heads to a book pasted together in Paris by six or seven ex-lawyers and ex-Jacobins?[49]

Karamzin's question showed not only his contempt for the French Revolution and anything to do with it, but his opposition to any foreign influence in Russia. He had also criticized Peter the Great for consulting foreign sources for many of his reforms and asserted that "the laws of a nation must be an outgrowth of its own ideas".[50]

Karamzin continued his criticism of Speranskii's plan on the issue of civil rights. He asserted that each class or estate in Russia had political rights according to its respective place in society while the French enjoyed civil rights for all before the law, which, directly challenged noble and autocratic authority. Whatever the merits of the case, Karamzin, de Maistre, and others influenced the emperor, and eventually Speranskii fell from power and was sent into exile.

Alexander dismissed Speranskii from his position as State Secretary in March 1812, partially because of his own personal peculiarities. Around the time of the invasion of Russia by Napoleon, Alexander began to exhibit rather odd personal behavior. He was seen less in public and for the rest of his reign he abandoned many of his early liberal reform ideas. For several weeks before his removal, Alexander had Speranskii watched, suspecting treason, and he feared that Speranskii's proposals, especially the "Plan of 1809," could infringe upon imperial privileges.

L.H. Jacob, a contemporary Prussian philosopher, political economist, and jurist, recounted first-hand the details of Speranskii's fall from power and offered his explanation of it. Jacob had come to Ukraine to teach at the University of Kharkov in 1806 after Halle had fallen to Napoleon. He taught there for three years and became well-known enough in St. Petersburg for his essays on the police and fiscal matters that Speranskii called for him to the capital to help with fiscal and legal reforms. He served on the Codification Commission and wrote a *Draft of a Criminal Code for the Russian Empire* in 1810. From late in 1809 until March 1812, Jacob worked closely with Speranskii mostly on the codification projects and established a good relationship with him.[51]

In March 1812, Jacob noted that Speranskii seemed unaware of his imminent fall from power, since he continued to work in his normal way before his arrest. Jacob wrote,

The generally known information was that on that day of his arrest, which occurred on an evening in March, 1812, Speranskii had reported to the tsar and, as usual, had with him a long discussion that lasted until upwards of 11 o'clock in the evening. On the way home he stopped off to see his friend, State Councillor Magnitskii, there discovered that the latter had been arrested and banished, went from their home, and met the police minister and a kibitka in front of his house. The police minister acquainted him with the tsar's orders; after having written a few notes and made a few other arrangements, and without wishing or being allowed to take leave of his sleeping daughter or mother-in-law, he stepped into the kibitka and escorted by a police officer, was taken at almost inhuman speed and discomfort to Nizhnii Novgorod.[52]

Jacob asserted that rumors began to circulate about Speranskii's arrest since few details were given by the emperor. Jacob believed that there were many possible causes for Speranskii's arrest and exile.

Speranskii insisted upon an examination to become a state councilor and alienated much of the nobility who lobbied with the emperor against Speranskii primarily on the basis of his social origins. The ministerial system that Speranskii had overhauled altered the hierarchy in each ministry. Speranskii made most officials report to the Council of State and not to the emperor as they had in the past. Many ministers were still reporting directly to the emperor as they had under the collegial system and blamed Speranskii for placing bureaucratic barriers between them and the emperor.[53]

Speranskii also reformed the functions of the Senate giving judicial power to the regional courts which bogged down with procedural delays reflecting poorly on Speranskii's otherwise noteworthy talents. Speranskii suffered as the scapegoat for the failure of this project even though many nobles and government officials worked hard to defeat it. Part of Speranskii's financial reforms was targeted at stabilizing the currency. He did so by halting the issuance of currency and the raising of taxes. The fiscal problems went back to the beginning of Catherine II's reign, but his plans were still unpopular. Without a doubt, though many Russian nobles, conservative, and others attacked Speranskii for his love things French. Many charged his with being a French agent under the control of Napoleon. While Speranskii was impressed with the *Code Napoleon* and used in his own legal drafts, there was no evidence that Speranskii would betray his country leaving these rumors unfounded. However, with the hysteria and rumors mounting Alexander sent Speranskii into exile.[54]

Speranskii's exile began in Nizhnii-Novgorod because Alexander did not want for his former advisor to be banished completely, but just far enough away from St. Petersburg to calm the fears Speranskii had generated. Speranskii left without his family, but they soon joined him. He was watched closely and despite his disgrace, conservative Moscow nobles, such as Count Rostopchin, continued to pursue Speranskii for harsher punishments. Even though Speranskii was not officially allowed to communicate with anyone in the capital, rumors circulated about his contact with friends through accommodating merchants who delivered messages for him. As Speranskii's unpopularity only intensified with the expansion of the war with Napoleon, Alexander felt that he had no choice but to send Speranskii farther away to Perm' in Siberia.[55]

In Perm', Speranskii was also a social outcast, had no official position, and even had difficulty finding a house. Alexander supplied him with an annual stipend of 6,000 rubles to support himself and his family. His daughter and mother-in-law had come lived with him in Nizhnii-Novgorod and even made the journey to Perm', but Speranskii sent his daughter and mother-in-law back to St. Petersburg so his daughter could receive a good education. As the defeat of Napoleon seemed assured, Alexander allowed Speranskii to move closer to the capital in the Novgorod province in mid-1814 and to return to government service after the signing of the Holy Alliance in 1815. Speranskii's image was improving and he, like many others in the Russian administration, believed that Alexander would return to the reform efforts initiated at the beginning of the century.[56]

During Speranskii's time in exile, he read widely on philosophy, law, and theology and studied foreign languages. He adopted the historical approach to law advocated by Prussian jurist Friedrich Savigny, who summarized his approach in the following passage:

> *In the earliest times to which authentic history extends, the law will be found to have already attained a fixed character, peculiar to the people, like their language, manners and constitution. Nay, these phenomenons have no separate existence, they are but the particular faculties and tendencies of an individual people, inseparably united in nature, and only wearing the semblance of distinct attributes to our view. That which binds them into one whole is the common convinction of the people, the kindred consciousness of an inward necessity, excluding all notion of an accidental and arbitrary origin.*[57]

   This attitude towards law would have its most profound impact on Speranskii's later codification efforts, but his legal writing after his return reflected a more mature and historical approach to law.

   Between 1818 and 1820, while in exile, Speranskii wrote an essay on natural law.[58] Speranskii claimed that people of a society must obey the natural order of the world because laws cannot be violated and it was a matter of conscience whether people would obey these laws. In other writings, Speranskii's legal thought evolved from one focused on natural law to a more historical approach. Speranskii asserted that "Theories that introduce natural law must draw from either [existing] principles, or from [existing] protections". He saw a direct link between natural law and the existing principles already present in society which would ultimately influence a nation's positive law. From his seminary education, Speranskii held fast to the notion that natural law was the source of all positive law, but he continued to wrestle with ideas on natural law and a more historical approach.[59]

   By the end of his exile, Speranskii had made a definite shift toward an historical approach to law. He proposed that "Legal theories emerging from internal protection of the power of our honor and conscience must be called virtuous [moral] legal theories (Jus morale)". He apparently abandoned the idea that legal theories originated in natural law and adopted the idea that the theories can develop out of social customs. He also claimed that "All good laws for men in society are the same as natural law; but not all of society's laws are able to be applied, and not all honor positivism".[60]

   In another essay written around 1820, Speranskii discussed law in a more general sense. He claimed that there were five basic areas of law; public, private, natural, foreign, and civil. The last, he claimed, was divided into five key categories: "1) fundamental laws, 2) estate laws, 3) police laws, 4) criminal laws [and] 5) ecclesiastical laws".[61] Speranskii claimed that this division was drawn directly from Roman law and despite Russia's rather unusual legal development, he tried to place its legal heritage in the traditions of ancient Rome. While Roman law influence nearly all European legal systems, Russia's, perhaps, was the one in Europe upon which it had the least influence.[62] For Speranskii, though, linking Russia to the legal heritage of ancient Rome and Europe in general was important. He was familiar with the legal traditions of Prussia, England, France, and Austria; and it was important to him to fit Russia into this mold. The easiest and politically safest way to do this was to link Russia with ancient Roman law.[63]

With the fall of the Western Roman Empire, Speranskii claimed that the legal heritage was transferred to Prussian and French areas and the systems that developed there by the time of the rise of Muscovy (1450) influenced the emerging Russian state.[64] However, Speranskii asserted that the Russian legal system, while linked to European systems, was derived primarily from a distinctly Russian legal development. He declared that the most profound documents of Russian legal history, including the *Sudebniki* of the fifteenth century and the *Sobornoe Ulozhenie (Law Code)* of 1649, were distinctly Russian documents that relied very little on outside influence.[65]

Speranskii credited the development of the modern legal system to the work of Peter the Great at the beginning of the eighteenth century. Peter had rationalized the legal and governmental systems in Russia along European lines, which Speranskii claimed, produced a distinct Russian legal system. Within this system, Speranskii identified several areas that were especially compelling. He believed that justice was the underlying basis for a strong legal system in Russia. Conversely, justice would survive only if there were a strong legal system. Speranskii believed that the two concepts of justice and unity were dependent upon each other for other to work. He realized later in his career that in Russia neither really existed. He asserted, then, that the people of Russia had to understand and believe in the legal system. Without this confidence, the system would not work. As part of this acceptance, Russians had to accept that laws were different according to estate as Speranskii had designed. Russians must also have faith in the benevolence of the government, in general, and the emperor specifically.[66]

Speranskii's conclusion about justice centered around the notion that if people embraced the general principles of law and believed that justice would prevail, then "all of those who received rationality and freedom from God were destined to obtain perfection". He concluded that until this perfection was reached, people had to rely upon one another and have faith in the system.[67] Speranskii's desire for perfection of Russia's legal system would last for the rest of his life. He had difficulty in his mission because of the generally illiterate Russian population and the lack of a real legal profession in Russia. Nearly all Russian jurists (which Speranskii was not) were trained abroad.

Even late in his career, Speranskii still strove for perfectibility. As he co-founded the Imperial School of Jurisprudence and began tutoring Grand Duke Alexander in 1835, he again addressed this notion of perfectibility. He instructed the young Grand Duke that law itself was a natural phenomenon given by God, and, in turn, man was responsible for the execution of God's will on earth. Similarly, he suggested that all humans were held together by a social bond, which is the highest expression of freedom and love.[68] Speranskii wrote

From this stems the true aspect of social life: it is the anteroom of higher existence – in it man prepares himself for the perfection of eternity.[69]

While many of Speranskii's ideas were consistent with those of various eighteenth-century European thinkers, he believed that the ultimate goal of freedom was the preservation of values and the perfection of society. He asserted that personal interests should be directed for the general good and not necessarily for personal gain. Speranskii wrote that

From this it follows that the error of those who construct everything on a balance of interests does not consistently recognize as a factor of action, but in their acceptance of these interests to the exclusion of everything else; they make interest the basis of social life or its ultimate aim; and they consider absolute good the concern of private morality and personal effort alien to social life, however, in reality without it all interests are means without ends, efforts without aims.[70]

Speranskii also believed that the connection between sovereignty and how laws were made needed to be clarified. He asserted that "the aims of legislation are: the preservation of being, the direction of all forces toward the truth, the direction of the will toward good, and the improvement of existence".[71] He further believed that the emperor should not direct legislation but should merely preserve and enforce "norms which have developed historically, and [direct] in the elimination of abuses and the correction of deficiencies in the light of the same historical tradition".[72] Raeff claims that "the course of lectures on law which he [Speranskii] read to Grand Duke Alexander is the ultimate expression of his political philosophy".[73] Indeed, it was clear from Speranskii's early writings at the end of the eighteenth century to this treatise on law just a few years before his death that he had matured and become more cautious in his legal thought. There seemed to be a clear division between his writings before his exile and those after. Evidently this time in exile allowed him ample time to ponder some of his more liberal ideas. As he gained government positions after Napoleon's defeat his writings become more conservative.

Speranskii's return to government service began with the governorship of Penza in central Russia, a first step, he thought, in his quest for full political recovery, despite the undesirable assignment. Speranskii soon learned that administering a backward provincial area was quite difficult since this area had remained unchanged for several centuries and his enlightened reform ideas were not immediately welcomed. In Penza, the educational levels were low and the strength of the local nobility was high. Raeff notes that Speranskii's success depended upon the land captain (ispravnik), a person well-respected in the community who Speranskii had to convince of the validity of his plans.[74]

Speranskii ruled Penza without incident. He made a good impression on the local nobility and on Alexander and balanced the budget of the province, but still experienced, as he had before and would again, the chronic problem of incompetent officials. Seeking to assemble groups of good bureaucrats for the work of local government reform, Speranskii believed sons of the clergy were a good source. He will return to this group for assistants in the Second Section under Nicholas I.[75]

Late in 1818 Speranskii, having decided to petition for reinstatement in St. Petersburg, wrote Alexander that he would retire completely from government service if he were not brought back to the capital. Alexander was not willing to lose such a valuable official so he sent Speranskii to Siberia where to administration was in disarray. Speranskii, not really ready to retire, took the assignment as a great challenge and a confirmation of his outstanding administrative abilities. He also thought that a successful reform of the chaotic Siberian system would result in a future position in St. Petersburg. Speranskii left for his undesirable assignment with broad powers from the emperor in 1819. Speranskii used local nobility in Siberia to begin the reforms. This province had suffered under the dictatorial rule of two previous governors the legacy of which was his immediate challenge.[76]

The primary accomplishment during his time in Siberia consisted of his statutes of 1821-22 to reorganize the local administration, which he approached with delicacy and tact by contacting many native tribes, including the Kazakhs and Buriats, before he began making changes.[77] Speranskii knew that Siberia held a wide variety of peoples with different religious, cultural, and social traditions; he was, nevertheless, interested in promoting Christianity throughout this diverse and vast province. In a letter to his daughter in 1821, Speranskii noted two key obstacles for reform and for the introduction of Christianity into Siberia. First, many native tribes, especially the Kazakhs, were wild in their festivals which left him skeptical about the possible introduction of Christianity, much less rational administrative reforms. Second, the Russian Orthodox clergy had, throughout the eighteenth century, tried to force their religion upon these tribes which left many of them with an instant aversion to Christianity. Speranskii encouraged the English Bible Society to work with many of the native tribes on educational, printing, agricultural, and spiritual matters. Since many natives felt less threatened by this approach, the English missionaries had their most profound influence in Siberia on education.[78]

Regarding the administrative reforms, Speranskii clearly understood that Siberia needed a clear, central, and hierarchical form of provincial government. He wanted to preserve local customs and traditions of the native tribes of Siberia if at all possible. He thought it was important to preserve the local autonomy of the native tribes while, at the same time, integrating them into the multi-ethnic Russian Empire. This appeared contradictory, but Speranskii advocated gradual integration through social and economic transformation rather than forced Russification that would only be met with resistance.[79]

Historian V.A. Riasanovsky notes that a lack of customary law and legal expertise left the native tribes without a functional administrative system, a problem that Speranskii's reforms of 1821-1822 were trying to correct and not necessarily to alter the existing power structure.[80] Speranskii outlined five areas for reform of the Siberian administration.

First, Speranskii did not think that issuing statutes that covered all of the tribes would work because each tribe had quite distinct social, religious, and cultural traditions. He proposed that these tribes be divided into three categories – settled natives, nomads, and vagrants – so reform could be implemented more efficiently. However, Speranskii and one of his assistants Gavriil Baten'kov did not make clear distinctions between the nomads and vagrants, as well as between the settled tribes and nomads. The general categories were used in the statutes, but none were defined adequately which left the reforms in a state of ambiguity.[81]

Second, since Speranskii felt that nomads and vagrants were less likely to adopt legal principles and procedures introduced from without, he established their administration based on their old customs. Speranskii had consulted mainly with settled tribes and much less with the nomads and vagrants. However, these customs were not well-defined nor uniform, so Speranskii tried to rationalize some of he local customs so they would be clearly defined and better organized. This contradiction plagued these reforms.[82]

Third, Speranskii worried about how to reform police functions. He had reformed the central administration's police during his earlier reform of the Ministry of Internal Affairs during the first years of Alexander's reign. In Siberia though, Speranskii left police matters in the hands of local nobility and the native tribes with the provincial government serving a merely advisory role. Speranskii feared that a heavy-handed approach would lead to revolt.[83]

Fourth, Speranskii advocated the protection of the freedom of trade and industry because he felt the only way to integrate these tribes fully into the Russian Empire was not by force or restriction, but by gradual means, where the tribes discovered for themselves the benefits of inclusion. Here again, Speranskii's adherence to the economic ideas of Adam Smith and others, influenced his provincial administrative reforms as far away as Siberia.[84]

Fifth, taxes had been a particularly sensitive subject for many tribes. Earlier they suffered under dictatorial administrators and were forced to pay exorbitant taxes. Speranskii designed a system that was based on the ability to pay. Each tribe was required to pay according to their means as a corrective measure for more than a century of high taxes that was often forced upon the tribes.[85]

While this statute seemed clear, the undefined status of settled tribes, nomads, and vagrants presented problems. Speranskii claimed that settled tribes were actually state peasants and were identified with the Russian peasantry except that local languages would be used for official purposes. The nomads and vagrants were even less clearly defined. In the statute itself, Speranskii reported eight features of the two groups without a real distinction emerging. The characteristics were

(1) uncertainty of place of residence; (2) level of civic education; (3) simplicity of customs; (4) particularity of customs (5) methods of finding substance; (6) lack of currency of exchange [and] (8) lack of means to sell the produce of their hunting and fishing on the spot.[86]

Clearly, these categories were extremely broad and again allowed for a great deal of ambiguity.

The full implementation of Speranskii's Siberian statutes proved to be slow and much of it was reversed during the reign of Nicholas I, but the reform helped bring Siberia more fully into the Russian Empire. This proved to be the most significant administrative development in Siberia from its absorption into the empire until 1917 and it showed how diligently and efficiently Speranskii could reform on a massive scale. While Speranskii's reforms maintained the rule of the Russian

Empire in the area, he had take some steps to help improve the position of the natives and worked hard to improve Siberia culturally, which continued after he left.[87]

Alexander summoned Speranskii back to the capital in 1821 on the heels of his administrative success in Siberia. Speranskii had proven his worth as a quality administrator and Alexander again utilized his talents by 1824. Now back in St. Petersburg, Speranskii, having learned his lesson earlier, was no longer aloof from St. Petersburg social circles. In fact, he made a more concerted effort to be sociable for his own career and for his daughter's future. Between 1822 and 1826, he served in a variety positions, became well-known in social and educated circles in St. Petersburg, and had close associations with several future Decembrists.

Late in November 1825, Alexander died in the Crimea, far from the capital, with no heir to take the throne. In 1822, Constantine, Alexander's brother, had renounced his right to throne leaving it in the hands of their youngest brother Nicholas. With this secret agreement and the peculiar circumstances of Alexander's death, the monarchy was vulnerable. In December 1825, and uprising of former military officers took place in St. Petersburg, Moscow, and other cities. The group known as "Decembrists" had many smaller factions with varied beliefs. One common thought was that the Russian monarchy in its current form could not longer continue. Most of the Decembrists were former military officers who felt betrayed by the resolution of the Napoleonic conflict and were irritated by the mysticism and lack of leadership exhibited by Alexander late in his reign.[88]

Nicholas took the throne and quickly crushed this uprising, but the far-reaching impact of the uprising was felt at very level of St. Petersburg society. Speranskii immediately came under suspicion because of his close association with several of the conspirators and his social acquaintance particularly with Nikolai Mordvinov, Nikolai Bestuzhev, Konstantin Ryleev, and Gavriil Baten'kov, with whom he was the closest.[89]

Baten'kov, originally from Siberia, had served in the campaigns of 1812-14 and the defeat of Napoleon where he was wounded badly and cited as a good officer. After his rehabilitation, he took a post in

Siberia as an engineer where he first met Sperankii in 1819 when the latter arrived as Governor-General of the province. Baten'kov served as Speranskii's quite capable assistant on the Siberian reform projects through which a good working relationship developed. Baten'kov's influence on and contribution to the Siberian reform legislation of 1821-22 was unmistakeable. Historian John Gooding describes the relationship between the two men as that of a father and son and Baten'kov as the pupil being taught how to be a bureaucrat and jurist by the master. With Speranskii's return to government service, many in and out of government respected both men for their legislative abilities as well as for their thinking on constitutional questions.[90]

Gooding notes that Speranskii's two years (1820-1822) in Siberia fostered a close intellectual relationship between the two men that continued in St. Petersburg. Baten'kov later noted that Speranskii wanted him to be "the heir to his unrealized thoughts".[91] When Speranskii was brought back to the capital in 1821, Baten'kov came with him, but the latter was assigned to work on the military colony project under General Aleksei A. Arakcheev. Both men were disappointed, but Baten'kov served his new master well. He continued, however, to formulate ideas on government and law, ideas that closely resembled Speranskii's, including elective consultative and legislative bodies for Russia that would not infringe on the powers of the monarchy. He, like Speranskii, advocated reform of the Russian government through gradual means, not revolution. The relationship between Baten'kov and Speranskii, including living in the same house in St. Petersburg, later linked Speranskii to the Decembrist uprising in 1825.[92]

The future Decembrists were interested in Baten'kov because of his ideas on constitutionalism, but seemingly more importantly, for his relationship with Speranskii. Gooding notes that while Speranskii's constitutional ideas were never publicly aired, copies of some of his writings were obtained by Nikolai Turgenev, and hence Speranskii became something of a martyr among revolutionaries for his being exile for his beliefs. Several of the Decembrists' plans included a temporary government of one to three people after overthrowing the monarchy. In this context, Speranskii's name was often mentioned, but most historians believe Speranskii knew nothing of these plans and, even if he had known, he would not have encouraged Baten'kov in such a radical course. Speranskii, after 1812, clearly had taken a more prudent political path and knew that an outright rebellion that failed would result in complete disgrace and probably execution. Above all, he was concerned still about his daughter's education and future.[93]

Once the uprising took place, Speranskii fell immediately under suspicion, but while the connection between Speranskii and the Decembrists was weak, it was there. As the events in St. Petersburg unfolded, Speranskii avoided the rebellion because of concern for his daughter, his family, and himself, and because he objected to revolution as a means of change. Many of the Decembrists, including Baten'kov, were disappointed with Speranskii's silence during the rebellion since they believed their cause mirrored much of what they thought Speranskii advocated. While there was some truth to their beliefs, Speranskii remained quiet and distanced himself even from his close friend, Baten'kov. Since the new emperor did not trust Speranskii, he decided to test his loyalty by appointing him to serve on the Commission of Enquiry in 1826, to see whether or not he could bring himself to prosecute the Decembrists.[94]

Speranskii accepted this duty with great pain and set about the process of investigating, prosecuting, and punishing the conspirators. Speranskii concluded that his friend Baten'kov agreed in principle with many of the Decembrists' constitutional ideas, but he did not march in Senate Square.[95] Nonetheless, Baten'kov was convicted and sentenced to one year in a Finnish prison and nineteen more in the Peter-Paul Fortress. His communication with Speranskii was cut off, and he did not even learn of his mentor's death in 1839 until years later. Undoubtedly, Speranskii saved Baten'kov from certain execution for his ideas and his refusal to sign a loyalty oath, and, in turn, Baten'kov's testimony downplayed the closeness of his relationship with Speranskii. According to Gooding, because Baten'kov had so much respect for Speranskii he did not want to tarnish his mentor's record, he testified that Speranskii was not involved in the planned uprising (which was true) and had no prior knowledge of it (which was still in question).[96]

Speranskii helped prosecute over five hundred people for this uprising. Nearly three hundred of these men were acquitted while over one hundred were identified as the most dangerous. Of these leaders, five were sentenced to be quartered while most others were sent to prison or exile. Nicholas had the five leaders hanged as a more humane punishment than quartering. The use of the death penalty was controversial because it had been officially outlawed under Catherine II. Some on the commission that passed the sentences thought they had been too lenient, while only one objected to the sentences. Speranskii apparently agreed with the sentences despite his associations with many of the conspirators.[97]

By July 1826, the Decembrist issue was finished for Speranskii as he had proved his loyalty and served the new emperor well. The next assignment would be the one Speranskii had desired since his return to public life in 1816 and one he regarded as the most challenging. Nicholas agreed that codifying Russian law was absolutely necessary. While to the Speranskii and Nicholas agreed on the necessity of having a new code of laws for Russia, their motivations for this project were very different.

NOTES:

[1] Marc Raeff, *Michael Speransky: Statesman of Imperial Russia, 1772-1839* (The Hague: Martinus Nijhoff, 1957), 1-5.

[2] Raeff, *Michael Speransky,* 1-3. Raeff's biography is the standard work in English on Speranskii's life. Unfortunately, the he was unable to use archival evidence for his biography. Other biographical works that will be used for this section are: M.A. Korf, *Zhizn' grafa Speranskago* 2 vols. (St. Petersburg, 1861); P. Romanovich-Slavatiskii, *"Gosudarstvennaia deiatelnost' grafa Mikhaila Mikhailovicha Speranskago* (Kiev, 1873); F.M. Dmitriev, "Speranskii i ego gosudarstvennaia deiatelnost'," *Russkii Arkhiv* 6 : 10 (1868) : 1527-1535; A. Fateev, *M.M. Speranskii* (Moscow, 1915); S.N. Ushakova, *M.M. Speranskii: Ego zhizn' i obshchestvennaia deiatelnost'* (St. Petersburg, 1891). For more information on Speranskii's association

with Freemasons, see Douglas Smith, *Working the Rough Stone: Freemasonry and Society in Eighteenth Century Russia* (DeKalb, IL: Northern Illinois University Press, 1999).

[3] Korf, *Zhizn'*, I, 37-65; Raeff, *Michael Speransky*, 9-13.

[4] F.M. Dmitriev, "Speranskii i ego gosudarstvennaia deiatelnost'," *Russkii Arkhiv* 6 : 10 (1868) : 1535-1540; Fateev, *Speranskii*, 11-14; Uzhakova, *Speranskii*, 11-15.

[5] Mikhail M. Speranskii, "Propoved 1791g.," *Russkaia Starina* 109 (February 1902): 283-91.

[6] Quoted in Marc Raeff, "The Political Philosophy of Speranskij," *American Slavic and East European Review* 12 : 1 (February 1953) : 4.

[7] Korf, *Zhizn'*, I, 272-80.

[8] Raeff, *Michael Speransky*, 20-23; Korf, *Zhizn'*, I, 67-80; Dmitriev, "Speranskii," 1357-41. Speranskii and Radishchev discussed many reform ideas in the brief time they served together on this commission. Apparently, the younger Speranskii was impressed with Radishchev's view of legality.

[9] Raeff, *Michael Speransky*, 17-19; "Samborskii, Andrei A.," *Russkii Biograficheskii Slovar'* 18 (St. Petersburg, 1896) : 147-55. This source will be referred to as *RBS* hereafter.

[10] Korf, *Zhizn'*, I, 80-89; Raeff, *Michael Speransky*, 20-28; Dmitriev, "Speranskii," 1541-45.

[11] David Marshall Lang, *The First Russian Radical: Alexander Radishchev, 1749-1802* (London: George Allen and Unwin, Ltd., 1959), 265-70.

[12] Janet Hartley, *Alexander I* (London: Longman, 1994), 1-81; Allen McConnell, *Tsar Alexander I: Paternalistic Reformer* (New York: Thomas J. Crowell, 1970), 12-13, 18-45.

[13] *Polnoe Sobranie Zakonov Rossiiskoi Imperii* 1st Series, xxvii, no. 20, 822 (July 1803). This source will be referred to as *PSZ* hereafter. Raeff, *Michael Speransky,* 50-53; McConnell, *Alexander I,* 68-79; Hartley, *Alexander I,* 58-94; Korf, *Zhizn',* I, 87-100; Daniel T. Orlovsky, *The Limits of Reform: The Ministry of Internal Affairs in Imperial Russia, 1802-1881* (Cambridge, MA: Harvard University Press, 1981), 20-30.

[14] Orlovsky, *Limits,* 20-21; *PSZ,* xxvii, no. 20, 852 (1803).

[15] David Christian, "The Political Ideas of Michael Speransky," *Slavonic and East European Review* 54 : 2 (April 1976) : 203; Mikhail M. Speranskii, "O korennikh zakonakh gosudarstva," in *Proekty i zapiski* ed. S.N. Valk (Moscow-Leningrad, 1961), 31.

[16] Speranskii, "O korennikh," 33-35; Christian, "Political Ideals," 204-06.

[17] Christian, "Political Ideals," 207.

[18] Raeff, "Political Philosophy," 11.

[19] Speranskii, "O korennikh," 31.

[20] Baron de Montesquieu, *Spirit of Laws* (New York: Colonial Press, 1900), I, Book 5, Chapter 14, 61; Melvin Richter, *The Political Theory of Montesquieu* (Cambridge: Cambridge University Press, 1977), -216.

[21] Speranskii, "O korennikh," 31-33.

[22] Peter Scheibert, "Marginelien zu einer neuen Speranskij-Biographie," *Jahrbucher fur Geschichte Osteuropas* 6 : 4 (1958) : 449-467.

[23] Raeff, *Michael Speransky,* 59.

[24] Ibid., 50-61; Richard S. Wortman, *The Development of a Russian Legal Consciousness* (Chicago: University of Chicago Press, 1976), 38-41.

25 Wortman, *Legal Consciousness,* 39-40.

26 J. Christopher Herold, *The Age of Napoleon* (Boston: Houghton Mifflin, 1963), 124-26.

27 Mikhail M. Speranskii, "Vvedenie k ulozheniu gosudarstvennikh zakonov (1809g.)," in *Plan gosudarstvennago preobrazovaniia grafa M.M. Speranskago* (Moscow, 1905), 1-120, and M.M. Speranskii, *Proekti i zapiski,* ed. S.N. Valk (Moscow-Leningrad, 1961), 143-221.

28 Speranskii, "Vvedenie," 168-74.

29 Wortman, *Legal Consciousness,* 43.

30 John Gooding, "The Liberalism of Michael Speransky," *Slavonic and East European Review* 64 : 3 (July 1986) : 401-10.

31 Quoted in Patrick A. Alston, *Education and the State in Tsarist Russia* (Stanford: Stanford University Press, 1969), 3.

32 Speranskii, "Vvedenie," 166-68; Raeff, *Plans,* 99-101.

33 Speranskii, "Vvedenie," 171.

34 Raeff, *Plans,* 104-108.

35 Speranskii, "Vvedenie," 185.

36 Raeff, *Michael Speransky,* 99-103; Korf, *Zhizn',* I, 187-220.

37 *PSZ,* xxxi, 24, 116 (February 1810).

38 Raeff, *Michael Speransky,* 102-05.

39 Korf, *Zhizn',* I, 251-70; Raeff, *Michael Speransky,* 102-105.

40 Raeff, *Michael Speransky,* 108.

41 *PSZ,* xxxi, 24, 686 (1811).

42 Raeff, *Michael Speransky,* 112-14; *PSZ,* xxxi, 24, 686 (1811).

43 Raeff, *Michael Speransky,* 115.

[44] N.M. Korkunov, *Russkoe gosudarstvennoe pravo* (St. Petersburg, 1909), I, 83; Speranskii, "Vvedenie," 1-35.

[45] Raeff, *Michael Speransky*, 50-75; Korf, *Zhizn'*, I, 272-90.

[46] David W. Edwards, "Count Joseph Marie de Maistre and Russian Educational Policy, 1803-1828," *Slavic Review* 36 : 1 (1977): 57-60.

[47] Ibid., 62-65.

[48] Ibid., 57-62.

[49] Richard Pipes, trans. and ed. *Karamzin's Memoir on Ancient and Modern Russia: A Translation and Analysis* (New York: Atheneum, 1966), 184.

[50] Pipes, *Memoir*, 185.

[51] David Griffiths and Karen Griffiths, trans. and eds., with intro. by Eduard Winter, "M.M. Speranskii As Viewed in L.H. Jacob's Unpublished Autobiography," *Canadian-American Slavic Studies* 9 : 4 (Winter 1975) : 520-50.

[52] Ibid., 533.

[53] Ibid., 535-40.

[54] Ibid., 533-39.

[55] Korf, *Zhizn'*, II, 80-92.

[56] Raeff, *Michael Speransky*, 185-203; Korf, *Zhizn'*, II, 46-90.

[57] Freidrich Karl Savigny, *Of the Vocation of Our Age for Legislation and Jurisprudence* trans. Abraham Hayward (London, 1831), 24.

[58] Mikhail M. Speranskii, "O prave estestvennom," Rossiiskaia Natsionalnaia Biblioteka, otdel rukopisei, F. 731: M.M. Speranskii, op. 1, d. 1266, 11. 1-8. This source will hereafter be referred to as RNB.

[59] Ibid., 7-8.

[60] Ibid., 8.

[61] Mikhail M. Speranskii, "O sisteme zakonov voobshche," RNB F. 637: K.G. Repinskii, op. 1, d. 806, 11, 1-2.

[62] Ibid., 2-3.

[63] Mikhail M. Speranskii, "O zakonakh rimskikh i razlichii ikh ot zakonov rossiiskikh," *Russkaia Starina* (1876): 592-97.

[64] Speranskii, "O sisteme zakonov," 5.

[65] Mikhail M. Speranskii, "Spravedlivost," RNB, F. 731: M.M. Speranskii, op. 1, d. 1320, 11. 1-6.

[66] Ibid., 1-5.

[67] Ibid., 4-5.

[68] Mikhail M. Speranskii, "O zakonakh: Besedy grafa M.M. Speranskogo Ego Imperatorskom Visochestvom Gosudarem Naslednikom Cesarevichem Velikam kniazem Aleksandrom Nikolaevichom s 12-go octiabria 1835 po 20 aprilia 1837 goda," *Sbornik Imperatorskogo Rosskago Istoricheskago Obshchestva* 30 (1881): 331-491.

[69] Quoted in Raeff, "Political," 15.

[70] Speranskii, "O zakonakh," 437.

[71] Ibid., 337.

[72] Quoted in Raeff, "Political," 17.

[73] Raeff, "Political," 17.

[74] Raeff, *Michael Speransky*, 190-200.

[75] Korf, *Zhizn'*, II, 113-60.

[76] Ibid., 125-55.

[77] *PSZ*, xxxviii, 29, 124-29, 134 (1821-1822).

[78] Marc Raeff, *Siberia and the Reforms of 1822* (Seattle: University of Washington Press, 1959), 287-95, 112-15; A.F. Bychkov, ed., *V Pamiat' grafa M.M. Speranskogo* (St. Petersburg, 1872), 198.

[79] Raeff, *Siberia*, 114-15.

[80] V.A. Riasanovsky, *Mongolskoe pravo – preimushchstvenno obychnoe* (Harbin, 1931), 230-32.

[81] Mikhail M. Speranskii, *Obozrenie glavnykh osnovanii mestnogo upravlaniia sibiri (po bumagum Speranskogo i sibirskogo komiteta 1821-1822* (St. Petersburg, 1841), 60-61.

[82] Ibid., 61.

[83] Ibid., 61.

[84] Ibid., 60-61.

[85] Ibid., 60.

[86] *PSZ*, xxxviii, 29, 126 (1822).

[87] Korf, *Zhizn'*, II, 164-200; Raeff, *Michael Speransky*, 260-280; W. Bruce Lincoln, *The Conquest of a Continent: Siberia and the Russians* (New York: Random House, 1994), 144-62; Raeff, *Siberia*, 53-128.

[88] For a full discussion of the Decembrist uprising, see Anatole G. Mazour, *The First Russian Revolution, 1825: The Decembrist Movement* (Stanford: Stanford University Press, 1937).

[89] John Gooding, "Speransky and Baten'kov," *Slavonic and East European Review* 66 : 3 (July 1988) : 400-02.

[90] Ibid., 400-05.

[91] Quoted in Gooding, "Speransky," 406.

[92] Gooding, "Speransky," 406-08.

[93] Ibid., 407-13.

[94] Mazour, *First Russian Revolution,* 203-221.

[95] Senate Square was where the uprising began and ended. The plan was to march on the Winter Palace and demand a constitution, but Nicholas' forces crushed it as it began.

[96] Gooding, "Speransky," 420-25.

[97] Mazour, *First Russian Revolution,* 210-15.

CHAPTER TWO

RUSSIAN CODIFICATION EFFORTS IN THE EIGHTEENTH AND EARLY NINETEENTH CENTURIES

Nicholas I charged Mikhail M. Speranskii with the duty of codifying Russian law. Speranskii and the Second Section of His Imperial Majesty's Personal Chancery (Vtoroe otdelenie sobstvennoi ego Imperatorskogo Velichestva Kantseliarii – hereafter Second Section) produced two massive volumes of laws; one an historical collection, *Complete Collection of Laws of the Russian Empire (Polnoe Sobranie Zakonov Rossiiskoi Imperii* – hereafter *PSZ*), and one a current digest of laws, *Digest of Laws of the Russian Empire (Svod Zakonov Rossiiskoi Imperii* – hereafter *SZ)*, published in 1830 and 1833 respectively. However, the Second Section was the eleventh commission since the era of Peter the Great called together to codify Russian law. Several of these earlier commissions influenced Speranskii's work and provided sporadic and incomplete lists of laws that helped the Second Section in their immense task.

All eleven codification commissions from 1700 to 1826 used the *Sobornoe Ulozhenie (Law Code)* of 1649 as its basis. The *Ulozhenie* was divided into twenty-five chapters, and each chapter contains numerous articles on such topics as "Blasphemers and Church Troublemakers," "Forgers and Those Who Counterfeit Seals," "Redemption of Military Captives," "Decrees on Atamans and Cossacks," and "The Musketeers."[1] These chapters each contained only a few articles, while several others have many more and so dominated the code. For instance, Chapter Ten addressed the "Judicial Process" in 287 articles. Likewise, Chapter Sixteen, "Service Lands," and Chapter Seventeen, "Hereditary Estates," have sixty-nine and fifty-five articles respectively. However, the *Ulozhenie* was best known for Chapter Eleven, "The Judicial Process for Peasants," which formally institutionalized serfdom in Russia.[2] This chapter formally institutionalized serfdom in Russia as many parts of Europe were freeing their bonded people. For the rest of the seventeenth century, the *Ulozhenie* served as the code of laws for the emerging Russian Empire with no major attempts to update or replace the code.

Soon after Peter the Great consolidated his power, he called the Office of the Code (Palata ob Ulozhenii) in 1700 to incorporate legislation from the last half of the seventeenth century into the *Ulozhenie*. In 1701, the Office completed its revision of legislation, but because of the outbreak of war with Sweden in late 1700, these revisions were not incorporated as planned, leaving Russian law in a continued state of chaos.[3]

In 1714, Peter again realized that the execution of the law in the Russian state was not uniform nor was it applied equally. He called together another commission to review the laws issued since the publication of the *Ulozhenie* in order to create a single compilation of Russian law, what he thought would lead to a uniform execution of the law. Again, this effort had few positive results.[4]

Later, in 1720, as war with Sweden was ending, Peter attempted to rationalize the Russian legal system and called on the Senate "to draft a Russian legal code along the lines of the Swedish and Danish codes, in particular."[5] Peter wanted to Senate to use the Swedish code of 1608 especially believing that this type of code would remove the arbitrary nature of Russian legal proceedings which was particularly evident during political trials. The Swedish historian, Claes Peterson, uses the term "code" in the Swedish sense and confirms that Peter would have welcomed an abstract code of laws for Russia, even though many later Russian rulers rejected the idea.[6]

Peter's immediate successors did little to alter the Russian legal system between 1725 and 1740. Soon after Elizabeth solidified her power in 1741, she directed the recently revitalized Senate to review all legislation issued during the previous fourteen years (1727-41) to be certain that during this "dark" (as Elizabeth called it) period there were no laws that contradicted Peter's "principles."[7] The Senate's work was slow and tedious and by 1750, only the laws issued during the first four of those years had been revised. Not surprisingly, perhaps as Evgenii Anisimov notes, the *PSZ* included more than 3,000 laws, dating from 1729 to 1741. Moreover, since Nicholas I omitted much legislative material from the draft of the *PSZ*, the amount of legislation reviewed by Elizabeth's Senate was undoubtedly far greater.[8]

By 1754, many in the Senate, including Peter Shuvalov, believed that a review of the past laws would not be of great benefit for Russia and Shuvalov proposed the writing of a new law code (ulozhenie) by a new commission to be created. Elizabeth agreed that a new law code was necessary to fit the changing times in Russia. The commission was created and by Elizabeth's death in late 1761, it had completed a section called "On the Status of Subjects in General." This document clearly showed that the economic and political power of the nobility was greater under Elizabeth, for it heavily influenced the contents of this code. Yet the events of 1761 and 1762 (Peter III's coming to power and quick fall) prevented this code from being completed and published.[9]

Elizabeth's codification commission lasted far beyond her death well into the reign of Catherine II. Speranskii later noted that a new commission was called during the first months of Catherine's reign, but it was simply a continuation of the Elizabeth's commission.[10] Its work continued until Catherine called her Legislative Commission of 1767. Shuvalov had dominated the first seven years of Elizabeth's commission, but the later years were controlled by senators like Roman Vorontsov. During Peter III's short reign, Vorontsov worked diligently to define the status of the nobility and their obligation of state service. Carol Leonard asserts that during Peter III's reign the effort to protect noble rights and privileges continued, as it did during Catherine II's reign.[11]

According to V.N. Latkin, however, the Elizabethan law code gave many more rights and privileges to the nobility than were granted under Catherine II.[12] Interestingly, Elizabeth had claimed to be the protector and inheritor of the Petrine legacy, but her law code clearly diminished the importance of the Table of Ranks and bolstered the power of the hereditary nobility. Anisimov found that her code even abolished compulsory state service for the nobility. Peter III later promulgated this provision, which was confirmed by Catherine II in the 1780s.[13] Latkin and Anisimov acknowledge that the distinctly pro-noble tone of Elizabeth's law code influenced Catherine's *Instruction (Nakaz)* to her Legislative Commission in 1767. In addition, Elizabeth's code basically granted the nobility monopolies over different industries like metallurgy and distilling. Moreover, though historians and jurists long ignored the status of the serfs in this code, this law code actually placed more restrictions of the serfs than did the *Ulozhenie* of 1649.[14]

Soon after Catherine II had solidified her power, she

issued a manifesto inviting all the free 'estates' of the realm and the central government offices to send deputies to the capital, empowered to explain the needs and problems of their communities, and to take part in the preparation of the new code of laws.[15]

This commission's composition differed from all previous legislative commissions since earlier groups had usually consisted of appointed nobles and officials, both foreign and domestic, but Catherine designed her Legislative Commission of 1767 to be representative of the various estates. Elected deputies brought petitions from the regions they represented that listed major legal and administrative problems and would be the basis for a new law code for Russia. However, the commission's role was still consultative; it was not empowered actually to enact law.[16]

Although it appears that Catherine's extraordinary Legislative Commission ended without meeting the goals of its convenor, that is not entirely true, because during its eighteen months of substantial work, the Commission debated several crucial issues. As mentioned before, the legal status of the nobility dominated many of the sessions, but the role of the middling classes and townspeople was also discussed. The last major issue, well-illuminated by the petitions brought by the deputies from the countryside, was the status of provincial administration. Even though, the Commission was dissolved when war broke out with Turkey in 1768, when Catherine later won the war (1774) and crushed the internal rebellion of Emelian Pugachev (1775), she used much of the information brought together by the Commission as the basis for such major legislation as the *Reform of Local Administration* of 1775, the *Charter to the Nobility* of 1785, and *Charter to the Townspeople* of the same year.[17]

One Russian jurist also seemed to have had a significant impact on Catherine's legal thought. Semion E. Desnitskii, who had studied with Adam Smith in Scotland in the Early 1760s, later submitted essays to Catherine for the reform of the structure of the Russian government and the Russian economy. Through Desnitskii, Catherine was exposed to the ideas of Baron de Montesquieu and Smith. Desnitskii first proposed the idea of three separate division of government based on Montesquieu, but with some alterations, granted more power to the executive.[18] Desnitskii also brought the economic ideas of Smith to Catherine's attention, particularly views on public finance expounded in chapter twenty-two of the *Nakaz* and through his influence she later added an appendix to her *Nakaz* concerning state economy.[19]

Desnitskii raised another critical point to Catherine concerning legal education in Russia. He was teaching law at Moscow University to a very small group of students, and there were still few properly-trained jurists in Russia. That he himself had been educated abroad was typical of anyone pursuing the law in Russia at this time, and he believed that with the immense work charged to the Legislative Commission, a body of trained jurists would certainly be necessary to assist it. Catherine agreed in principle, but failed to take any concrete, long-lasting steps to promote legal education in Russia. It was not until 1835, that the Imperial School of Jurisprudence opened in St. Petersburg, Russia's first institution dedicated exclusively to the study of law. Ultimately, this Commission illuminated two glaring deficiencies in Russia's legal system: the need for a complete compilation of all the laws of the Russian Empire and the need for a domestically-trained legal profession.[20]

Only in the last decade of Catherine's reign (1785-1796) was the Senate assigned the duty of drafting a new law code, among its other newly assigned roles, and in 1796, when Catherine died, the Senate still had not completed the work. Paul expanded the duties and size of the Senate, as he did nearly every aspect of the Russian governmental system and quadrupled its size, enabling it to work more efficiently. However, by the end of his brief reign (1801), the work of codification was still incomplete. In 1805, Paul's son and successor, Alexander I, expanded the Imperial bureaucracy to more than 10,000 people and reinvigorated the work of codifying Russian law, thus setting the stage for the codification efforts of Speranskii which began as Nicholas I took the throne in 1826.[21]

Early in Alexander's reign, the new emperor recognized the necessity for legal reform in Russia. Having endured the reactionary and chaotic policies of his father, Paul, Alexander desired a clear set of laws for the efficient administration of the empire. Paul had called together a commission to codify Russian law in 1797 primarily to reverse many of the policies of his mother, Catherine II. Alexander reorganized his commission in August 1801, and placed long-time imperial bureaucrat P.A. Zavadovskii at the head of the commission.[22] Zavadovskii had served both Catherine and Paul in several positions; however, most of the members of this commission were not jurists. Alexander instructed Zavadovskii on the principles by which this commission should be based.[23]

Alexander, always being heavily influenced by his grandmother Catherine II, used the provisions she laid down in her *Instruction (Nakaz)* to the Legislative Commission of 1767-68.[24] He wanted his commission to follow these more than five hundred guidelines for codification work, conduct, and etiquette. He also wanted Zavadovskii and this commission to analyze all of the plans of the former commissions of the eighteenth century, beginning with those of Peter the Great. From these older plans the emperor wanted the commission to determine the general principles of Russian law. This was a common duty for nearly every previous commission, but it was never successfully accomplished. It required an in-depth knowledge of the law, and it also rested on the assumption that general legal principles existed in eighteenth-century Russia.[25] Alexander wanted all laws in the Russian Empire, both foreign and domestic to be considered in the development of general principles for the codification process. In the end, though, Alexander insisted that plans and proposals had to be approved by him personally.[26]

Alexander Radishchev was the most notable person on this commission. His more liberal reform efforts were often frustrated by the more conservative Zavadovskii. In his brief tenure on this commission, he and Speranskii became friends and often agreed on constitutional questions. Radishchev's library contained Jean-Jacques Rousseau's *Du Contrat Social*, William Blackstone's *Commentaries on the Laws of England*, and Adam smith's *Wealth of Nations* which clearly influenced three of the documents he authored for the commission. However, after Radishchev's suicide, the work of this commission lagged badly and was forced to abandon its original mission of collecting all existing laws.[27]

Prince P.P. Lopukhin suggested that the commission simply establish some basis principles of Russian law, a suggestion which created a controversy in the commission and at court. Zavadovskii and several other members of the commission disagreed with Lopukhin's plan, but his idea for a more theoretical approach appealed to Alexander and the members of his "Unofficial Committee." Because of this disagreement and a recognition of Zavadovskii's inept leadership, he was replaced temporarily with a member of Alexander's "Unofficial Committee," N.N. Novosil'tsev.[28]

The commission was reorganized again in 1804 and fell under the direction of Baron Gustav Rosenkampf. However, he, too, was unprepared for such work. Rosenkampf was a Baltic German who knew little of "Russian law, Russian conditions and even Russian language."[29] The new director did not want to establish an abstract code of law for Russia. Rather, he proposed the historical approach with sought to preserve local customs while establishing a body of law for the whole empire. Despite the efforts of these first two commissions during Alexander's early reign, the work was not progressing as quickly as the emperor would have liked. Alexander also began to feel uncomfortable in allowing the commissions to determine a legal code, despite his espousal of such liberal ideas. In 1808, Alexander had grown tired of the slow pace of the work and appointed a new head of the commission, Assistant Minister of Justice Speranskii, to reorganize and direct the work of this commission. Speranskii took the position and believed that the codification efforts

earlier in Alexander's reign were the first serious work of codification
since Catherine's Legislative Commission.[30]

Alexander appointed Speranskii to this position because he knew
of his administrative talents, but Speranskii did not have any formal
education in law. He often remarked on the sad state of present and
past Russian laws and looked to foreign models because he felt that
there were no domestic examples worth exploring. The most recently
drafted European law code was the *Code Napoleon*. Speranskii used
this code and other European codes as models when he drafted his
"Plan of 1809." Speranskii provided legal principles, usually from
foreign legal models, and the staff was required to find appropriate
Russian laws to fit the principles. Speranskii was more interested in
establishing a code of Russian law that would be the basis for future
constitutional plans.[31]

Karamzin openly attacked Speranskii's plan for being a direct
translation of the France's *Code Napoleon* noting several instances
where Speranskii directly adopted passages from the French code.
Karamzin also invoked nationalistic sentiments for his preservation of
the Russian legal tradition; with the increasing tension with Napoleon,
he saw this not only as a legal problem, but a patriotic one as well.
When Speranskii took control of codification efforts in 1826, he agreed
with Karamzin's historical approach to codifying and collecting
Russian law. Karamzin approved of Speranskii's later plans and told
him "this is what I have always been preaching" just weeks before the
noted historian died.[32] However, as Speranskii was sent into exile in
1812, he always felt that his ideas from 1809 were misunderstood. He
wrote to Alexander from Perm' trying to regain access to St. Petersburg
as well as explain what his "Plan of 1809" really meant.[33] Speranskii
claimed that his reliance on the French code was justified because of
the common legal heritage France and Russia shared from ancient
Roman law. He further claimed that Alexander had been misinformed
by people like Karamzin and others concerning the nature of his plan.
In this letter to the emperor, Speranskii stressed the direct legal
connection to ancient Roman law especially concerning the ministries,
senate, and civil law. He even claimed that many parts of the *Code
Napoleon* were drawn directly from Roman law promulgated by
Justinian.[34]

With Speranskii in exile after 1812, the work of the commission fell again under the control of Rosenkampf. He wound remain the head of the Commission on Laws until the Second Section was created in 1826. During the Napoleonic wars, though, the work of the commission ceased, but with victory and resolution at the Congress of Vienna in 1815, Rosenkampf and the commission had resumed work on a journal and a systematic survey of the laws. The *Journal of Legislation (Zhurnal Zakonodatel'stva)*, which appeared in 1817 and 1819, and whose publication was suggested by the chief administrator of the Commission, Lopukhin, in August 1817, addressed in its first issue the question of law during the reigns of Anna and Catherine II. Lopukhin viewed this journal as a vehicle for instructing the public and government officials about past and current Russian laws. In that first volume, however, there was no attempt to rearrange the laws of these two reigns chronologically or alphabetically, so it was difficult to find specific laws. The laws were just generally listed by reign. The Commission recognized that this arrangement made it difficult to locate specific laws. In late 1817, and early 1819, the commission published a supplement to the 1817 volume, which provided dates and a chronological arrangement to make laws more accessible.[35]

The Commission published all of the laws issued by the Senate and by imperial decree. It provided complete lists of laws for 1817 (319), 1818 (253), and 1819 (260). In 1819, independent of the *Journal of Legislation*, the Commission proposed the publication of another journal called the *Critical Journal of Russian Legislation (Kriticheskii zhurnal Rossiiskogo zakonodatel'stva)* to address large theoretical questions of law in its pages rather than just catalog past and current laws of the Russian Empire. Even though the work was completed for this journal, it was not published because it did not gain the proper number of subscriptions to offset the fifteen kopecks per page publication costs.[36]

Rosenkampf attributed the failure of this second law journal to the writings of jurist Alexander P. Kunitsyn in another periodical. Kunitsyn, a professor of law and philosophy at the newly-formed St. Petersburg University, published an article in *Son of the Fatherland (Syn Otechestva)* entitled "On Constitutionalism."[37] He proposed more radical ideas on constitutionalism than those being currently discussed during Alexander's reign. Kunitsyn was greatly influenced by the writings of Jean-Jacques Rousseau. Rosenkampf believed that Kunitsyn, through his provocative writings, had focused legal and philosophical debates in the pages of *Son of the Fatherland* and *Spiritual Journal (Dukh Zhurnalov)*; the latter which was published by Nikolai Grech and usually published a conservative response to Kunitsyn's proposals.[38]

Even though the *Critical Journal* was never published, the Commission had still provided valuable legal information for the years just after the defeat of Napoleon. Between 1815 and 1822, the Commission published the *Systematic Survey of the active laws of the Russian Empire with the foundations of law derived from them (Sistematicheskii svod sushchestvuishchikh zakonov Rossiiskoi Imperii s osnovaniiami prava iz onykh izvlechennymi)*.[39] The survey was intended to serve as an active code of laws for Russia.

This survey required Rosenkampf to send many of his assistants to archives in St. Petersburg and Moscow in order to collect all of the laws of the empire. The Commission began publishing these laws in successive volumes starting in 1815 and eventually produced fifteen volumes by 1822. The *Systematic Survey* contained nearly 30,000 laws promulgated from the *Law Code* of 1649 to 1818. Through the accumulation of this material, Rosenkampf tried to discover the basis for the rationale for Russian law which proved to be a daunting task because the legislation from the late seventeenth, eighteenth, and early nineteenth centuries did not have any rational order. Anyway, the laws that were published were divided into different categories and arranged chronologically in each section. While the *Systematic Survey* was never the active code of law for Russia, it did serve as a major source for Speranskii's later codification efforts.[40]

In the first volume of the *Systematic Survey*, Rosenkampf outlined the general principles of the collection. Rosenkampf tried to determine the source of each law collected. Most laws were issued by the monarch, but his assistants discovered that many laws were promulgated by the Senate while others were issued by local governments in the provinces. This was the one problem that plagued previous commissions and would persist during Speranskii's later work beginning in 1826. While Rosenkampf organized all of the administrative laws together, civil laws though secular in nature, were examined to make sure each one adhered to the general principles of Russian Orthodoxy.[41]

Rosenkampf directed several assistants to examine the issues of crime and punishment while collecting these laws. One of the first questions centered around what exactly constituted a crime in the Russian Empire and whether or not it was criminal or civil. A second question was what constituted a proper defense. The assistants found references to laws that referred to representation in defense cases, but no clear picture of a proper defense appeared during the Commission's work. The assistants provided Rosenkampf with numerous laws that remedied "transgressions against the general peace."[42]

Rosenkampf designed provisions for general principles of Russian jurisprudence. Only one section focused on the running of the state while others dealt with the material of the royal family, the morality of the youth, and the guidelines for education, but financial issues dominated this party the survey. Most of the financial provizions focused on state revenue, but many others were centered on expenditures, budget revisions, shipping laws, allotments, custom houses, and agricultural and industrial endeavors.[43]

This list of categories in the *Systematic Survey* in which Russian law was classified represented all the laws in effect in the Russian Empire between 1815 and 1822. However, there were many mistakes, omissions, inconsistencies, and prejudices in how the *Systematic Survey* was compiled and what was ultimately included and what was not. In 1830, when Speranskii begins work on the *Digest of Laws (Svod Zakonov* or *SZ)*, his assistants fell victim to the same problems leaving this active code of law in Russia in 1833 suspect. After the appearance of the last volume of the *Systematic Survey* in 1822, Balug'ianskii and Speranskii began to take a larger role in the Commission. Just a few months before the death of Alexander in 1825, Balug'ianskii and Speranskii set the priority for the Commission to be the accumulation of all laws since the *Law Code* of 1649. They began to reorganize laws into three broad categories. Civil laws occupied three chapters.

Commercial laws, which included laws on trade conducted by the Russian government and on bankruptcy who the second category. The last category was criminal laws. Speranskii and Balug'ianskii became much more active on the Commission after the completion of the *Systematic Survey* while Rosenkampf was little more than a figure head.[44]

After learning of Alexander's death in the Crimea in late November 1825, Speranskii began to petition the new emperor, Nicholas I, to create a new codification commission. He delivered his first petition on December 12, 1825, in the midst of the Decembrist rebellion.[45] Speranskii continued to petition Nicholas in January 1826, requesting the eleventh commission since 1700 created for the purpose of codifying Russian law. Nicholas created the Second Section of His Imperial Majesty's Personal Chancery to codify Russian law with Balug'ianskii as its director. The Second Section replaced the Commission on Laws that had been under the direction of Rosenkampf for more than a decade. Nicholas kept this group in his personal chancery so he could monitor its composition and activities, but he allowed Balug'ianskii (the official head) to select the staff himself which included such liberal figures like Speranskii, Kunitsyn, and others.[46]

Nicholas I created the Second Section in January 1826, in order to codify Russian law for the first time since the Law Code of 1649. Blug'ianskii immediately called upon his long-time colleague Speranskii to work with him in the Second Section. Early in the Second Section's work, Speranskii assumed most of the real duties in the commission while Balug'ianskii attended to the more formal activities despite the fact that the latter was one of the few trained jurists in the Second Section. Speranskii, since his exile, had adopted a new approach to law. Early in his career, he relied heavily on foreign legal models for the creation of abstract legal principles for Russia. While in exile Speranskii read widely and became more politically prudent, especially under the more conservative Nicholas. He adopted the historical approach to law that was advocated by Prussian jurist, Friedrich Savigny.[47] Speranskii proposed three projects for the Second Section in early 1826.

First, he wanted the Second Section to collect and publish all legislation of the Russian Empire from and including the *Law Code* of 1649 until the death of Alexander I in 1825. With the immense and ever-changing geography of the Russian Empire from the mid-seventeenth to the early nineteenth century, the variations and often contradictions in law from the provincial areas to the heartland of Russia. Also, what exactly constituted a law was in question. The source of law in Russia was also complex, especially for laws from the eighteenth century. Speranskii, Nicholas I, and most of the members of the Second Section saw this mainly as an historical exercise, to put the past laws in chronological order so that the commission could address its other tasks.[48]

Second, Speranskii wanted the Second Section to draw up a digest (svod) of all the laws currently in effect in the Russian Empire. He designed this work to rely heavily on the work of the historical collection as well as previous commissions. The digest was intended to serve as the basis for the emerging modern legal profession, and judges would have a body of laws to refer to in handing down decisions.[49]

The third proposal was to draft a new abstract code of law for Russia. This had not been accomplished since 1649, but Speranskii felt that all of the groundwork had been laid and a new code could be quickly drafted. Nicholas agreed to the first two proposals, but not the third. He wanted a clear set of current laws from which he could rule. He was not necessarily as interested in the historical collection, but Speranskii defended it as necessary for the creation of the current digest. Nicholas definitively denied the third proposal for an abstract code because it would have been a restriction on his absolute power. Having come to power in the midst of a revolt, Nicholas did not want anything to jeopardize his power. Speranskii and Balug'ianskii accepted Nicholas decision on the abstract code and began work on the other two projects by May 1826.[50]

Soon after the Second Section was together, Speranskii began to send assistants all over the empire in an attempt to collect all of the laws of the empire. This project presented Speranskii and Nicholas with tremendous financial concerns. To travel throughout the empire would be an expensive undertaking. Speranskii again experienced the same problem of unprepared personnel for highly technical work. Speranskii ideally wanted to spread assistants all over the empire to collect laws from all possible depositories, but this task was too immense. Within the first weeks of the Second Section, Speranskii abandoned the full-scale search for laws and limited the scope of the search.[51]

Under Alexander I, P.M. Stroev had begun to collect laws and statutes from across the empire, but his collection was far from complete. Speranskii used his fragmentary beginnings and built upon them. Speranskii ideally did not want to rely on the work of previous commissions because of their limitations, prejudices, and omissions. However, he soon realized that in order to collect all of the laws for the past 175 years from all over the empire, he would have to rely on these previous efforts. By early 1828, Speranskii limited the search for eighteenth century laws to the Senate archives in St. Petersburg and virtually ignored the collections in other archives in St. Petersburg and most of those in Moscow as well. Speranskii received lists of laws with brief abstracts from assistants in Moscow from which he selected certain laws to be added to the collection based solely on the titles and brief abstracts.[52]

Speranskii realized that many of the assistants he sent to regional archives and other depositories were unprepared for such a technically sophisticated undertaking. Within the first few months of the work of the Second Section, it became clear that most of the work would fall on Speranskii's shoulders. However, there were four other members of this commission who served as core of jurists for the work at hand. Balug'ianskii, who was the official head, Alexander P. Kunitsyn, a purged professor, Modest A. Korf, later biographer of Speranskii, and K.I. Arsenev.

The men involved in the work of the codification of Russian law in the Second Section had diverse family backgrounds, educations, and careers. Certainly Speranskii's life before 1826 had taken him through a series of career changes for better and worse, as we have seen. Like Speranskii, there were men in the Second Section who were sons of parish priests. Others were of noble birth who pursued careers in civil service for a variety of reasons. Educational levels varied among the members of the Second Section. Only a few were trained jurists, but most were well-educated in a variety of fields like Speranskii. The career patterns of the members varied quite a lot as well. Some were older men toward the end of their careers like Speranskii. For some this commission was the culmination of a lifetime of work for legal reform in Russia. Others were young men who were just starting their careers and later helped with legal reforms under Alexander II.

From 1826 to 1833, the membership of the Second Section changed frequently, however there were a few members who provided a stable foundation. Speranskii,[53] as discussed earlier, was the driving force behind the codification work. The following discussion will focus on the family backgrounds, educations, and careers of four key members of the Second Section who played crucial roles in the production of the *PSZ* and *SZ* in 1830 and 1833 respectively.

The end of Alexander I's and the beginning of Nicholas I's reign was a time when the Russian Empire had reached its greatest geographic dimensions and incorporated many peoples not of purely Russian origins. One good example of this was the head of the Second Section, Balug'ianskii. He was born in 1769 to a Carpatho-Russian family of Slavic origins who professed the Uniate faith. His father was a fairly prominent local official in the village of Olshava and his mother was from Russian peasant origins, but converted to the Uniate faith when she married. Balug'ianskii represented the multinational nature of the Russian bureaucracy in the nineteenth century.[54]

Aside from Speranskii and Balug'ianskii, Kunitsyn was probably the most important member of the commission. He worked from its origins in 1826 until the early 1830s when he took on other duties in the government. Kunitsyn, though, was not of high or foreign birth. His father was a parish priest in the Tver' region. Kunitsyn was born there in 1783 and had to prove his intellectual worth in order to be sent to the local seminary. Even though he was younger than Speranskii, his background and early education resemble that of the *de facto* head of the commission.[55]

Modest Andreevich Korf was born in 1800 and served in the Second Section under Speranskii. His father was of German origin and his mother was Russian. Korf's grandfather had gained hereditary noble status during the reign of Catherine II. Korf's father had been educated abroad and was able to rise to the head of the College of Justice under Paul I and later to be a senator in 1819. Korf's father saw the value in education and civil service so he directed his son down this same path. Because of his family background, a career in civil service for Korf was certain.[56]

The last of the four was Konstantin I. Arsenev. He was somewhat more obscure than the others, but his role in the commission was significant. He was born in 1789 in the Kostroma Province where his father was a parish priest. Like Kunitsyn, he was able to gain advanced education by proving his intellectual abilities at an early age. Clearly, the members of the Second Section were from a variety of backgrounds which would definitely determine the course of their respective educations and careers.[57]

Balug'ianskii's educational background before attending Vienna University was somewhat vague. He lived at home until he was eight years old. His father taught him Latin at home until he entered the gymnasium where he was exposed to theology and moral sciences. From there he was sent to the Korolevskii Academy of Jurisprudence in Kosha to study in the philosophy faculty, which he completed with the highest honors.[58]

Balug'ianskii then attended Vienna University and studied law. He completed his undergraduate studies in 1789. He completed his doctorate in law in 1796 and took a position at Pest University. His education in Vienna was especially important because he was there during the opening phases of the French Revolution. During the revolution, he denounced the liberal ideas of the philosophies and became known as a leading conservative. He was also exposed to the freemasonry movement which was growing in Europe and only beginning in Russia. He became a prominent member of a freemason society where he and other members of the group discussed all of the current revolutionary ideas coming out of France. In addition, he became critical of religious dogmatism and fanaticism. It was also clear from the curriculum he followed at Vienna University that he studied the works of Montesquieu, Voltaire, Rousseau, Helviticus,

Renali, and Mably, but Adam Smith's ideas on political economy particularly appealed to Balug'ianskii. He was also exposed to a variety of legal philosophies that would prove useful in his later codification work. These philosophies included German historical law, natural law and Roman law.[59]

Kunitsyn pursued his education in several different steps. He began his education at religious schools in the Tver' region. His father also introduced him to theological studies as he entered the Tver' Seminary. He finished his studies in 1803 and had performed so well that he was allowed to attend the Pedagogical Institute in St. Petersburg. He stayed there for five years and was chosen by his teachers to study abroad. He attended the University of Göttingen for about a year and a half where he studied law, philosophy and moral sciences. He also spent about nine months at the Universities of Heidelberg and Paris. His studies there were less academic. He spent most of his time in pursuit of a young woman. In 1811, he returned to Russia and took a position at the recently opened lyceum at Tsarskoe Selo.[60]

While abroad Kunitsyn had been exposed to and adopted many of the philosophical ideas put forth by Kant and Rousseau. Exposure to these philosophies would influence his teaching and later publications. Also, while he was in Göttingen, he became friends with a fellow Russian student, Nicholas Turgenev. The two often debated the most popular intellectual topics of the day. Turgenev was noted by professors as the keener of the intellects and would eventually be involved in the Decembrist Uprising in 1825.[61]

Korf took a distinctly different path in his education. Since he was of noble birth, he qualified for admission to the lyceum at Tsarskoe Selo. He began his studies in 1811 and he stayed there for six years. In that time, he took courses from Kunitsyn, but was not impressed with his instruction, while most students loved the young teacher and flocked to his courses. During his time at the lyceum, he took classes on religion, political history, mathematics, geography and foreign languages. In later years, Korf focused on law and Alexander I proclaimed that an education at the new school equaled that of a university education. Whether or not this was true remains unclear, but what was certain was that through this school service to the state and loyalty to the emperor was constantly pronounced. Upon graduation from the lyceum, Korf began work in the Ministry of Justice in 1817.[62]

Arsenev's early education resembled that of Kunitsyn. He worked through local religious schools and instruction from his father until he was ten years old. From 1799 to 1806, he excelled at the Kostroma Seminary. Because of his academic excellence, he was able to attend the Pedagogical Institute in St. Petersburg for four years. As he finished his education, he took a position teaching at the Muralt Pension, a preparatory school for Russian noble children in St. Petersburg, where he began to make many friends in the Russian imperial court which would prove beneficial later in his career.[63] Even though all of these men had different family and educational backgrounds, their careers would all meet in 1826 in the Second Section. For the most part, their careers had been in academia and civil service.

Balug'ianskii began his teaching career at Pest University in 1796 where he taught history, statistics, and public law. In 1804, upon the invitation of the "Unofficial committee" member, Novosil'tsev, he took a position at the St. Petersburg Pedagogical Institute. Soon after he arrived, Balug'ianskii began to work on the Commission on the Laws with Rosenkampf and Speranskii. Among his many pressing concerns early in his career were the conditions of the peasantry. He first addressed this in 1816-17 when he worked on a commission called together to analyze the condition of the peasantry in Livland. Later, he composed a two-volume work for Alexander outlining how to emancipate the serfs.[64] He also worked on commissions concerned with the treasury, debt, credit, law and police. His talents were many and Alexander used them to their fullest extent.[65]

Beginning in 1813, Balug'ianskii tutored Grand Duke Nicholas. In 1817, he became director of the St. Petersburg Pedagogical institute which would become St. Petersburg University two years later. He continued as the first rector of this new university during the transition. In 1821, a purge of liberal professors took place at the new university which left Balug'ianskii in an awkward position. There were thirty-two professors when the university opened in 1819. Novosil'tsev recruited seasoned and published scholars to fill these positions which resulted in the assembly of quite a distinguished faculty in St. Petersburg. There was also a group of young, liberal scholars who pushed the bounds of toleration.[66]

The governor of Simbirsk, Mikhail Magnitskii, reported to the conservative Minister of National Enlightenment, Alexander Golitsyn, that the recently opened university in Kazan was filled with liberal and radical professors. Magnitskii purged the university of these evil elements. This frightened Golitsyn and so he began to investigate the professors at St. Petersburg University. He turned this investigation over to the head of the Central School Board, D.M. Runich. He attacked the teaching and writings of many professors including Kunitsyn and Arsenev as heretical and removed them from their positions at St. Petersburg University in 1821.[67]

Balug'ianskii defended his faculty members from these attacks, but could not save their jobs. He resigned his position in protest in 1821. Ironically, because of his earlier tutoring of Grand Duke Nicholas, he continued to serve as one of the future emperor's closest advisors. Finally, just after the Decembrist Uprising in 1825, he and Speranskii proposed a commission to Nicholas that would codify Russian law. In January 1826, Balug'ianskii was placed at the head of this new commission, the Second Section. It was evident that his early conservative leanings and private tutoring of the royal family helped secure him the position as the head of the eleventh commission (Second Section) called to codify Russian law since 1700.[68]

Kunitsyn's career was more academic and less service-oriented. He took a position at the lyceum at Tsarskoe Selo in 1811. He taught a wide variety of courses and generally received high acclaim for his courses. He was honored several times in the poetry of his most famous student, Alexander S. Pushkin. The poet often attributed his own thinking on legal matters to the instruction he received from Kunitsyn.[69]

In 1817, Kunitsyn began teaching at the Pedagogical Institute. He stayed on when the school became St. Petersburg University in 1819. As mentioned earlier, Kunitsyn was one of a handful of professors at the university who were expelled in 1821 for liberal leanings. Runich raised charges against several faculty members for their teaching and writing. In Kunitsyn's case, his new two volume work, *Natural Law*

(Pravo Estestvennoe), published in 1818 and 1820, gave Runich and ammunition he needed to remove Kunitsyn. Runich charged Kunitsyn with promoting the heretical ideas of Western thinkers like Rousseau, Kant, and Smith. Kunitsyn's teachings and writings were at the center of this controversy. Runich labeled Kunitsyn's writing as "pseudo-thinking" and the work of an "enemy of God."[70]

However, Kunitsyn taught several jurists who were outraged by his dismissal. Kunitsyn was also accused of providing seditious ideas for his students. Dmitri Zamiatnin, who studied under Kunitsyn at the lyceum, later became a prominent player in the judicial reforms under Alexander II. Richard Wortman claims that Zamiatnin's writings from his schooldays revealed that Kunitsyn gave "detailed summaries of Russian law and procedure and the history of Russian criminal law, with citations of legislation since the law code of 1649."[71] Another former student of Kunitsyn's would also take part in the judicial reforms in the 1860s was Alexander Gorchakov. A complete set of his lecture notes from Kunitsyn's classes at the lyceum were published in *Krasnyi Arkhiv* in the 1930s. This lengthy publication of Gorchakov's notes confirmed the notion put forth in Zamiatnin's writings. Kunitsyn provided a thorough and detailed explanation of Russian law from the mid-seventeenth century through the early legal efforts of Speranskii. Also, Gorchakov defended Kunitsyn against his critics who purged him from the university. Despite these defenses and high acclaim, Kunitsyn lost his position.[72]

After his removal from St. Petersburg University, Kunitsyn continued to teach law and other subjects privately between 1821 and 1825. He taught several young men who would later take part in the Decembrist Uprising in 1825. During the interrogations in early 1826, several Decembrists mentioned Kunitsyn as the inspiration for their constitutional thought. Interestingly, no charges were brought against Kunitsyn. In fact, he was quickly appointed to the Second Section in 1826 where he served until the early 1830s. Balug'ianskii personally asked for Kunitsyn to be appointed to this commission, and also brought many other of the former professors purged from St. Petersburg University to serve in the Second Section.[73]

Much of Korf's and Arsenev's careers actually were after their time in the Second Section. Korf was selected by Speranskii to work under him in the Ministry of Justice in 1817. He then was selected to work in the Second Section in 1826 and served there until 1833 when he took a position in the Committee of Ministers. He later became a State Secretary and was assigned the task of writing a history of Russia's central administration. He never finished this work, but he had become one of Russia's most knowledgeable officials.[74]

By 1840, Korf moved in the highest political and social circles in St. Petersburg. In 1848, revolutions gripped Europe and Korf took this opportunity to try and replace S.S. Uvarov as the Minister of National Enlightenment. He claimed that Uvarov had neglected his censorship duties. He was unsuccessful in removing Uvarov, but his views on censorship won him appointment to the Menshikov Committee, later the Buturin Committee in 1848. He served in this position until 1855. He realized that stricter censorship only resulted in more underground activity and further dissent. Once Alexander II came to power, the new emperor quickly abolished the committee.[75]

Korf was held in high regard by Nicholas I. He had tutored Grand Dukes Konstantin and Mikhail and lectured widely and law and jurisprudence. In 1849, Korf was appointed director of Imperial Public Library in St. Petersburg which was once administered by the Ministry of National Enlightenment. It suffered from poor leadership, but Korf reorganized it, increased its funding, and bought many valuable collections, including that of Mikhail Pogodin's manuscripts in Old Church Slavonic.[76]

In 1861, Korf resigned as head of the library to become head of the Second Section. He played a key role in the discussions of the Zemstvo reform of 1864. He also published a two-volume biography of his mentor, Speranskii, in 1861. This biography stood as the standard work on the bureaucrat until the appearance of Raeff's biography in 1957.[77] From there, he was appointed to the Council on Laws were he remained until 1872. He died in 1876.[78]

Arsenev's career before the Second Section was brief. As mentioned earlier, he taught briefly at the Muralt' Pension, then at the Pedagogical Institute in 1817. He taught at the Engineering Academy in 1818. In that same year, he began to publish books on geography and statistics.[79] The following year he taught at the Pedagogical Institute which was quickly reorganized as St. Petersburg University. In 1821, he lost his position, like Kunitsyn, in the purge of the university by Runich. He was eventually exonerated by Nicholas in 1827. He tutored the future Alexander II and taught in the Engineering Academy. From 1826 until the early 1830s, he was appointed to the Second Section where he served under Speranskii and Balug'ianskii. After his service in the Second Section, his career was more distinguished. He published two historical works on Peter II and Catherine I.[80] He also discovered Karamzin's "Memoir on Ancient and Modern Russia." He did not publish it, but it circulated in intellectual circles. From 1835-53, he served as head of the State Statistical Administration. He contributed to many statistical studies of the Russian Empire during this time. Arsenev was one of the founders of the Russian Geographic Society in 1845. The society's early studies focused on the peasantry and Arsenev contributed much statistical information to this subject. Arsenev's most famous work was his *Statistical Sketches of Russia (Statisticheskii ocherki Rossii)*, published in 1848. He was criticized for its impracticability and for dedicating it to the future Alexander II. He had been critical of the current condition of the peasants and thought that the future emperor agreed. However, the current emperor, Nicholas I, did not agree and all copies were recalled and a new dedication was inserted. He suffered no other punishment. By the early 1850s, he had reached the height of his career. He had attained the rank of Privy Councillor (3rd on the Table of Ranks) and was the recipient of numerous academic and service awards. He died in November 1865 in Petrozavodsk.[81]

Aside from Speranskii, these were the four key members of the Second Section who directed much of the work that produced the *PSZ* and the *SZ*. In the following sections, it will become clear how these men and Speranskii compiled these massive collections and how their own backgrounds, educations, and careers influenced how they carried out their tasks. These are also the men who were primarily responsible for supervising and teaching the assistants in the Second Section.

NOTES:

[1] Richard Hellie, trans. and ed., *The Muscovite Law code (Ulozhenie) of 1649* (Irvine, CA: Charles Schlacks, Jr., Publisher, 1988), I, vii-ix.

[2] Ibid., 85-94.

[3] Claes Peterson, *Peter the Great's Administrative and Judicial Reforms: Swedish Antecedents and the Process of Reception* (Stockholm: A.B. Nordiska, 1979), 306; V.N. Latkin, *Zakonodatel'nye kommissii v Rossii v XVIII st.* (St. Petersburg, 1887), 1-18; M.M. Bogoslovskii, "Palata ob ulozhenii 1700-1703 gg." *Izvestiia AN SSSR* 15-17 (1927) : 1347-1474; 1 (1928) : 81-110.

[4] Peterson, *Peter the Great's Administrative*, 306-07; Latkin, *Zakonodatel'nye Kommissii*, 18-20.

[5] Peterson, *Peter the Great's Administrative*, 307-08.

[6] A.S. Zamuruev, "Priemy i metody kodifikatsii pri podgotovke proekta ulozheniia rossiiskogo gosudarsta v 20-e gody XVIII v," in M.P. Iroshnikov, et. al., eds., *Vspomopatel'nye istoricheskie distsipliny* 25 (1994) : 118.

[7] Evgeny V. Anisimov, *Rossiia v seredenie XVIII veka: Bor'da za nasledie Petra* (Moscow: Mysl', 1986), 43-45; Latkin, *Zakonodatel'nye kommissii*, 20-21.

[8] Anisimov, *Rossiia*, 43-50.

[9] Ibid., 48-50; Latkin, *Zakonodatel'nye kommissii*, 22-24.

[10] Mikhail M. Speranskii, *Obozrenie istoricheskikh svedenii o Svod Zakonov* (St. Petersburg, 1833), 4-6.

[11] Carol S. Leonard, *Reform and Regicide: The Reign of Peter III of Russia* (Bloomington, IN: Indiana University Press, 1993), 48-56.

[12] Latkin, *Zakonodatel'nye kommissii*, 24-28.

13 Evgeny V. Anisimov, *Empress Elizabeth: Her Reign and Her Russia, 1741-1761,* trans. John T. Alexander (Gulf Breeze, FL: Academic International Press, 1995), 55-65.

14 Ibid., 57-65.

15 Isabel de Madariaga, *Russia in the Age of Catherine the Great* (New Haven, CT: Yale University Press, 1981), 139.

16 Ibid., 140-41.

17 Ibid., 182-84.

18 S.E. Desnitskii, "Proposal for the Establishment of Legislative Judicial, and Executive Power in the Russian Empire," in *Russia Under Catherine the Great: Volume I: Selected Documents on Government and Society,* ed. and trans. Paul Dukes (Newtonville, MA: Oriental Research Partners, 1978), 47-68.

19 Madariaga, *Age of Catherine of Great,* 155-65; Paul Dukes, "Introduction," in *Russia Under Catherine the Great,* 44-46.

20 A.H. Brown, "Adam Smith's First Russian Followers," in *Essays on Adam Smith,* eds. Andrew S. Skinner and Thomas Wilson (Oxford: Oxford University Press, 1975), 269-73; A.H. Brown, "S.E. Desnitsky, Adam Smith, and the *Nakaz* of Catherine II," *Oxford Slavonic Paper* 7 (1974) : 42-50; Desnitskii, "Proposal," 59-63.

21 Roderick McGrew, *Paul I of Russia, 1754-1801* (Oxford: Clarendon University Press, 1992), 219-20.

22 *PSZ,* xxvi, 19, 989 (1801).

23 P.M. Maikov, *Vtoroe otdelenie sobstvennoi ego Imperatorskogo Velichestva Kantseliarii 1826-1882* (St. Petersburg, 1906), 1-100; Marc Raeff, *Michael Speransky: Statesman of Imperial Russia, 1772-1839* (The Hague: Martinus Nijhoff, 1957), 66-70.

24 Empress Catherine II, *The Grand Instructions to the Commissioners Appointed to Frame a New Code of Laws for the Russian Empire: Composed by Her Imperial Majesty Catherine II Empress of All the Russias*, trans. Michael Tatishcheff (London: T. Jeffreys, 1768).

25 P.M. Maikov, "Kommisii sostavleniia zakonov pri imperatorakh Pavle I i Aleksandre I," *Zhurnal Ministerstva Iustitsii* (December 1905):273-75.

26 Ibid., 276.

27 David M. Lang "Radishchev and the Legislative Commission of Alexander I," *American Slavic and East European Review* 6 (1947): 7-13.

28 *PSZ*, xxvii, 21, 187 (1804); Maikov, "Kommisii," (September 1905): 85-91; (November 1905): 236-50; A.E. Nolde, *Ocherki istorii kodifikatsii metnykh grazhdanskikh zakonov pri grafe Speranskom* (St. Petersburg, 1906), I, 45-58; Raeff, *Michael Speransky*, 70-74.

29 Raeff, *Michael Speransky*, 67.

30 *PSZ*, xxx, 23, 525, (1808); Mikhail M. Speranskii, "Kratkoe istoricheskoe obozrenie kommisii sostavleniia zakonov," *Russkaia Starina* 15 (1876) : 433.

31 Raeff, *Michael Speransky*, 68; Maikov, "Kommisii," (November 1905) : 240-65; Nolde, *Ocherki*, 58-68.

32 Richard Pipes, trans. and ed. *Karamzin's Memoir on Ancient and Modern Russia* (Cambridge, MA: Harvard University Press, 1959), 81-83, 182-90.

33 Mikhail M. Speranskii, "Permskoe pismo Speranskago k Imperatoru Aleksandru I," in *Plan Gosudarstvennago Preobrazovaniia grafa M.M. Speranskago* (Moscow, 1905), 328-35.

34 Mikhail M. Speranskii, "O zakonakh rimskikh i razlichii ikh ot zakonov rossiiskikh," *Russkaia Starina* 15 : 6 (1876) : 434-41.

[35] Raeff, *Michael Speransky*, 321-25; Maikov, *Vtoroe*, 87-90; Mikhail M. Speranskii, *Obozrenie istoricheskikh svedenii o Svod Zakonov* (St. Petersburg, 1833), 34-40.

[36] Maikov, *Vtoroe*, 89; Speranskii, *Obozrenie*, 2.

[37] Alexander P. Kunitsyn, "O konstitsii," *Syn Otechestva* 45 (1818) : 202-10.

[38] Barry Hollingsworth, "A.P. Kunitsyn and the Social Movement in Russia under Alexander I," *Slavonic and East European Review* 43 (1964) : 114-29; Kunitsyn, "O konstitsii," 202-08.

[39] Maikov, *Vtoroe*, 89; Hollingsworth, "Kunitsyn," 114-25.

[40] Maikov, "Kommisii," (December 1905) : 189-200; Maikov, *Vtoroe*, 78-87; Raeff, *Michael Speransky*, 321-30; Modest A. Korf, *Zhizn 'grafa Speranskago* (St. Petersburg, 1861), II, 69-79.

[41] "Zhurnal Kommisii sostavleniia Zakonov," May 31, 1822, Rossiiskii Gosudarstvennii Istoricheskii Arkhiv, F. 1251: M.M. Speranskago, op. 1, d. 51a, 11. 82-83. This archive will hereafter be referred to as RGIA.

[42] Maikov, *Vtoroe,* 78-87; Korf, *Zhizn ',* II, 269-75; "Zhurnal Kommisii sostavleniia Zakonov," May 31, 1822, RGIA F. 1251: M.M. Speranskago, op. 1, d. 51a, 11. 82-84.

[43] Maikov, *Vtoroe*, 78-87; "Zhurnal Kommisii Sostavleniia Zakonov," June 3, 1822, RGIA F. 1251: M.M. Speranskago, op. 1, d. 51a, 1. 82.

[44] Maikov, *Vtoroe,* 110-12; "Zhurnal Kommisii Sostavleniia Zakonov," June 21, 1822, RGIA, F. 1251: M.M. Speranskago, op. 1, d. 51a, 11. 94-95; "Zhurnal Kommissii Sostavleniia Zakonov," May 9, 1822, RGIA, F. 1251: M.M. Speranskago, op. 1, d. 51a, 1, 73.

[45] See Chapter 1 for a discussion of Speranskii's role in the Decembrist uprising.

[46] Raeff, *Michael Speranskii*, 321-25; Maikov, *Vtoroe,* 110-15; Speranskii, *Obozrenie*, 42-65.

47 Raeff, *Michael Speranskii*, 322-28; Friedrich Karl Savigny, *Of the Vocation of Our Age for Legislation and Jurisprudence,* trans. Abraham Hayward (London, 1831), 17-49.

48 Raeff, *Michael Speransky,* 321-30; A. Filippov, "Speranskii kak kodifikator russkogo prava," *Russkaia Mysl'* 10 (1892) : 195-221; *PSZ* 2nd series, 1, (1825); "Predislovie," *PSZ,* (1830), v-xxv.

49 Ibid., xx-xxv.

50 Ibid., v-xx; Richard Hellie, trans. and ed., *The Muscovite Law Code (Ulozhenie) of 1649* (Irvine, CA: Charles Schlacks, Jr., Publisher, 1988), I, xv-xxv; W. Bruce Lincoln, *Nicholas I: Emperor and Autocrat of All the Russias*, (DeKalb, IL: Northern Illinois University Press, 1978), 100-103.

51 Richard S. Wortman, *The Development of a Russian Legal Consciousness* (Chicago: University of Chicago Press, 1976), 7-89.

52 Maikov, *Vtoroe*, 116-45; Wortman, *Legal Consciousness,* 30-59.

53 See Chapter 1 of this study for Speranskii's biographical information.

54 "Balug'ianskii, Mikhail Andreevich," *Russkii Biograficheskii Slovar'* 2 (St. Petersburg, 1896) : 451-55. Hereafter will be referred to as *RBS*; "Balug'ianskii, Mikhail Andreevich," *Modern Encyclopedia of Russian and Soviet History* 3 (Gulf Breeze, FL: Academic International Press, 1977): 61-62. Hereafter will be referred to as *MERSH*; E.M. Kosachevskaia, *M.A. Balug'ianskii i Peterburgskii Universitet pervoi chetverti XIX veka* (Leningrad, 1971), 3-35; P. Baranov, *Mikhail Andreevich Balug'ianskii: Stats-sekretar, Senator, tainii sovetnik, 1769-1847* (St. Petersburg, 1882), 1-10; "Proekt sudebnago ustroistva M.A. Balug'ianskago," in *Sbornik Statei N.M. Korkunova, 1877-1897* (St. Petersburg, 1898),134-40; A.N. Fateev. *Akademicheskaia i gosudarstvennaia deiatelnost M.A. Balug'ianskago (Balud'ianskago) v Rossii* (Moscow, 1971), 1-20.

[55] "Kunitsyn, Alexander Petrovich," *RBS* 9 (St. Petersburg, 1896): 551-52; Hollingsworth, "Kunitsyn," 114-20; I. Seleznev, *Istoricheskii ocherk Imperatorskago byshago tsarskosel'skago nyne Aleksandrovskago Letseia za pervoe ego piatidesiatiletie s 1811 po 1861 god* (St. Petersburg, 1861), 44-59.

[56] Wortman, *Legal Consciousness*, 41-45; Raeff, *Michael Speransky,* 350-54; "Korf, Modest Andreevich," *RBS* 8 (St. Petersburg, 1896): 440-43; O.D. Golubeva, *M.A. Korf* (St. Petersburg, 1995), 7-50; "Korf, Modest Andreevich," *MERSH* 17 (Gulf Breeze, FL: Academic International Press, 1976): 109-112.

[57] Wortman, *Legal Consciousness,* 253-54; "Arsenev, Konstantin Ivanovich," *MERSH 2* (Gulf Breeze, FL: Academic International Press, 1976) : 109-112.

[58] Kosachevskaia, *Balug'ianskii,* 3-50.

[59] Baranov, *Balug'ianskii,* 1-10; Fateev, *Akademicheskaia,* 1-20.

[60] Hollingsworth, "Kunitsyn," 114-28; Markus Wischnitzer, *Die Universitat Göttingen und die Entwicklung der liberalen Ideen in Russland im ersten Viertel des 19. Jahrhunderst* (Berlin, 1907), 34-39; V. Valdenberg, "Priroda i zakon v politichskikh vozzreniiakh Pushkin," *Slavia* 4 : 1 (1925) : 69-81.

[61] F.N. Smirnov, "Kunitsyn i dekabristi," *Voprosy Istorii* 6 (1967): 216-18; Thomas Nemeth, "Kant in Russia: The Initial Phase (Cont'd)," *Studies in Soviet Thought* 40 (1990): 316-22.

[62] "Korf," *RBS* 8 (St. Petersburg, 1896): 440-43; Wortman, *Legal Consciousness*, 41-45; Maikov, *Vtoroe,* 116-45; Allen A. Sinel, "The Socialization of the Russian Bureaucratic Elite, 1811-1917: Life at the Tsarskoe Selo Lyceum and the School of Jurisprudence," *Russian History* 3 : 1 (1976): 1-31.

[63] "Arsenev," *MERSH 2* (Gulf Breeze, FL: Academic International Press, 1976): 109-12; Wortman, *Legal Consciousness*, 253-54.

[64] E.M. Kosachevskaia, "Krest'ianskie proekty M.A. Balug'ianskogo," *Istoriia SSSR* 6 (1970): 83-94.

[65] Kosachevskaia, *Balug'ianskii,* 3-50; Baranov, *Balug'ianskii,* 1-14; Fateev, *Akademicheskii,* 1-25.

[66] Kosachevskaia, *Balug'ianskii,* 47-100; Fateev, *Akademicheskii,* 25-40; Baranov, *Balug'ianskii,* 20-45.

[67] Whittaker, "From Promise to Purge," 148-67.

[68] Baranov, *Balug'ianskii,* 25-40; Whittaker, "From Promise to Purge," 148-65.

[69] V. Valdenberg, "Pushkin i Kunitsyn," *Slavia* 14 : 3 (1937): 321-28.

[70] Whittaker, "From Promise to Purge," 155-65; Hollingsworth, "Kunitsyn," 119-28.

[71] Wortman, *Legal Consciousness,* 41, 72.

[72] Whittaker, "From Purge to Promise," 150-65; James T. Flynn. *The University Reform of Tsar Alexander I, 1802-1835* (Washington, D.C.: Catholic University Press, 1988), 184-85; A.M. Gorchakov, "Litseiskie lektsii," *Krasnyi Arkhiv* 80 (1937): 75-120.

[73] Hollingsworth, "Kunitsyn," 117-26; M.V. Nechkina, *Dvizhenie Dekabriskov* (Moscow, 1955), II, 231.

[74] Golubeva, *Korf,* 7-45; "Korf," *RBS* 8 (St. Petersburg, 1896): 440-43; "Korf," *MERSH* 17 (Gulf Breeze, FL: Academic International Press, 1980): 177-80; Wortman, *Legal Consciousness,* 195.

[75] "Korf" *RBS* 8 (St. Petersburg, 1896): 440-43.

[76] Golubeva, *Korf,* 10-65.

[77] Modest A. Korf, *Zhizn' grafa Speranskago* 2 vols. (St. Petersburg, 1861) and Marc Raeff, *Michael Speransky: Statesman of Imperial Russia, 1772-1839* (The Hague: Martinus Nijhoff, 1957).

[78] "Korf," *RBS* 8 (St. Petersburg, 1896): 440-43; "Korf," *MERSH* 8 (Gulf Breeze, FL: Academic International Press, 1980): 177-80.

79 Konstantin I. Arsenev, *Kratkaia vseobshchaia geografiia* (St. Petersburg, 1818) and *Nachertanie statistiki Rossiiskago gosudarstva* (St. Petersburg, 1819).

80 Konstantin I. Arsenev, *Tsarstvovanie Petra II* (St. Petersburg, 1839) and *Tsarstvovanie Ekateriny I* (St. Petersburg, 1856).

81 "Arsenev," *MERSH* 2 (Gulf Breeze, FL: Academic International Press, 1967): 109-112; N.P. Nikitin, "K.I. Arsenev i ego rol v razvitii ekonomicheskoi geografii v Rossii," *Voprosy geografii* 10 (1948): 3-40.

CHAPTER THREE

PURPOSE AND COMPILATION OF THE POLNOE SOBRANIE ZAKONOV ROSSIISKOI IMPERII AND THE SVOD ZAKONOV ROSSIISKOI IMPERII

In late 1829, as the Second Section completed its work on the *PSZ*, Speranskii drafted his "Preface" to the work. Archival evidence shows that Speranskii went through several drafts before he completed the preface.[1] He outlined very clearly the causes and purposes of this collection. Speranskii examined the history of codification efforts from Peter the Great to Alexander I and discovered, that after the Ulo*zhenie* of 1649 was issued by Tsar Aleksei Mikhailovich little legal work took place before the height of Peter I's reign in the early eighteenth century.

By 1710, Peter had promulgated numerous decrees and laws. During his entire reign he issued thousands of laws, including the *General Regulation* (1720) and the *Ecclesiastical Regulation* (1721), for example. By 1720, it was evident to Peter that all of these laws needed to be organized in some way. In April, 1720, Peter instructed the Senate to appoint a group of officials to collect and publish the laws of his reign. The group was only able to publish some of the laws as they did not have the resources or the training to complete the task. This was just one example of the many attempts during the eighteenth century to collect some or all of the laws of the Russian Empire. However, several of these efforts produced small, incomplete collections of laws from specific periods, as just mentioned with respect to Peter I. Speranskii used several of these collections in his codification work, but he also invoked their incomplete nature, and sporadic appearance as a partial justification for the *PSZ* in his proposal to Nicholas I in early 1826.[2]

During Alexander I's reign, codification efforts became more organized, systematic and successful. Soon after assuming the throne in 1801, Alexander brought together a legislative commission, but it was not until after the conflict with Napoleon that the commission began to produce substantial material. Between 1817 and 1820 they published the *Journal of Legislation (Zhurnal Zakonodatel'stva)*, in several volumes. This journal contained sporadic lists of laws promulgated during the previous two centuries. Speranskii maintained that this was one of many collections the Second Section reviewed during their work on the *PSZ*. A survey of the whole journal reveals two things. First, this collection contains laws from the *Ulozhenie* of 1649 to the early nineteenth century. Second, this collection is focused primarily on a twenty-seven year period divided between the reigns of Peter the Great and Catherine the Great.[3] It was a good starting point for Speranskii, but it also strengthened his argument for a complete collection.

Speranskii and the Second Section utilized more than ten popular journals, government periodicals and legal publications from the late eighteenth and early nineteenth centuries. Some of these publications were *St. Petersburg Messenger (Sanktpeterburgskii Vestnik)* (1778-1781), *St. Petersburg Senate Bulletin (Sanktpeterburgskii Senatskiia Vedmosti)* (1809-1829) and the *Sistematic Survey (Sistematicheskii Svod)*, of 1821.[4] Using these sources as well as fresh archival and library research conducted by members of the Second Section, Speranskii believed that he could provide a complete edition of the laws of the Russian Empire. However, he soon realized that the *PSZ*, as it was being published between 1828 and 1830, had several incomplete sections and was flawed with many errors related to textual accuracy and the origins of laws.

As the work of the Second Section began in early 1826, Speranskii faced several pressing questions. First, what would be the scope of this collection? Many previous commissions had begun the work of codification after the *Ulozhenie* of 1649, as examined previously, but Speranskii believed that later legislation was connected to this early code so it should be include. The end point was more problematic. Speranskii debated between Alexander I's death (November 19, 1825), the day Nicholas I took the throne (December

12, 1825), or the end of 1825, near when the Second Section began its work. The rest of the collection was arranged by reign so Speranskii concluded the *PSZ* with the day that Nicholas I took the throne.[5]

The second important question was to define what a law in Russia was between 1649 and 1825. Russia had not had the same legal development as most of Europe had. Russia had been ruled by an autocracy for several centuries, and the role of law had always been seen as identical with the wishes of the monarch. However, during these 176 years (1649-1825) it was clear that laws and legal consciousness came from a variety of sources. One of the first problems was the stark differences in law and how it was understood and administered throughout the Russian Empire. Ethnic, religious, linguistic, and cultural differences across the empire made uniform enactment and enforcement of the law difficult. Many of the Western territories also made claims to a legal tradition other than Russia's. They felt that they should be treated separately in the codification process, but only the Baltic areas received special consideration.[6]

Speranskii realized quickly in 1826 that the source of Russian law in the past 176 years was not simply the monarch. Besides the regional differences, Russian laws had been issued from a number of sources like the Senate, the Imperial court, and provincial governors depending upon the reign.[7] Additionally, all laws were not issued in the same way or stored in the same places. Speranskii first considered the Senate archives in St. Petersburg to be the main depository for laws, but he soon learned that many laws were held at other archives in both St. Petersburg and Moscow. He also discovered that the published lists of laws from earlier commissions were incomplete. By spring 1826, he understood that for a full collection to be compiled a thorough investigation of the archives, libraries, and government offices of St. Petersburg and Moscow would have to be completed.[8]

However, Speranskii was not a trained jurist, and even though Balug'ianskii and several other members of the Second Section were, the task of deciphering the source of every law to determine its validity seemed impossible. During the spring of 1826, Speranskii limited the scope of the project to those laws issued by imperial decree *(ukaz)*. This meant that only laws coming directly from the monarch's hand or in his or her name would be included in the *PSZ* with a few exceptions. With this one act, Speranskii radically altered the nature and scope of this endeavor.[9] Historians and jurists since have criticized Speranskii for his rather arbitrary decision. However, the following discussion will show that Speranskii faced many obstacles and he made this practical choice rather than suffer the same fate of previous legislative commissions.

With the scope of the project defined, Speranskii addressed the question of where he would obtain the laws. He began this project with the idea to cover all archives and libraries in Moscow and St. Petersburg, if not all of the empire. Since Speranskii had limited the inclusion of laws to those issued by the monarch or in his or her name, the scope of the search was greatly limited. The Second Section never numbered more than thirty members at any time under Speranskii's direction, and most of these men were well-educated, but few in law. As a result, it was difficult to send these assistants to distant locations in search of certain kinds of laws. Most were not capable of exercising such discretion, therefore regional archives, libraries, and government institutions were virtually ignored except for those in the Baltic areas.[10]

After only a few months, the search focused on only a few depositories in St. Petersburg and lists from archives in Moscow. In St. Petersburg nearly all of the work was conducted in the Senate archives while others such as the War College, State Archives in Moscow were only sporadically surveyed. Speranskii and Balug'ianskii corresponded with officials from these institutions in Moscow concerning lists of laws that were being sent to the Second Section for review. Between 1826 and 1830, Speranskii went to Moscow at least once personally to supervise the work. He found that the most valuable material in the Moscow archives was from the period between 1649 and 1711. Obviously, once Peter the Great moved the capital to St. Petersburg in 1711, most official documents were stored there.[11] Speranskii then turned his attention to the incomplete lists and collections assembled by previous commissions.

Most previous commissions arranged their collections topically. The *PSZ*, however, was arranged chronologically because Speranskii thought this would make it easier to use. When the work was divided between the members of the Second Section, however, it was not so simple. Speranskii had the senior members, and in turn the assistants, carried out their work topically. He did this in preparation for the *SZ*. Many, including Speranskii, considered the current digest to be more important than the historical collection. Speranskii divided the work between his main five members, Alexander Kunitsyn, Modest Korf, Konstantin Arsenev, Gustav Zimmerman, and Dmitri Klokov. These members were in charge of the distribution of their work, and they supervised the work of their assistants.[12]

The section on civil law was directed by Zimmerman while Klokov and Kunitsyn directed the work on personal and imperial law. Arsenev and Korf worked on commercial and administrative law respectively. Speranskii apparently divided this work according to the senior members' areas of expertise. The senior members delegated much of the work to their assistants. So, each member worked on their particular topic over 176 year period covered in the *PSZ*.[13] Even though the *PSZ* was an historical collection, Speranskii thought that it should be continuously updated. This topical approach proved valuable for the organization of the *SZ*.

After nearly four years of work on the *PSZ*, Speranskii turned his attention to the current digest, *SZ*. Speranskii outlined in the "Preface" to the first series of the *PSZ* published in 1830 that there would be two collections. The first collection would "begin with the *Ulozhenie* of 1649 and conclude on December 12, 1825."[14] The items to be included in this first collection would be all laws *(zakony)* and decrees *(ukazy)* issued by the autocrat. The second collection or series would begin where the first one left off and the first volume would end in 1830. After 1830, a volume would be produced to cover every year. Speranskii realized that keeping an accurate and current list of laws on an annual basis would be much easier than the task he and his assistants had just completed.

Speranskii further explained why this collection came first and why it included only those laws issued by the monarch. He and other members of the Second Section believed strongly that the only way to compile an accurate digest of current laws for Russia was to compile all the laws from Russia's past first. From this historical basis, it would be easier to determine what should be included in an active code of laws.[15] Another principle Speranskii outlined in the "Preface" was a little more complicated. While the laws included were restricted to

those issued by the monarch, Speranskii did allow under certain
circumstances for judicial decisions related to imperial decrees to be
included. In most cases, though, these decisions were merely
refinements of the decree and not contradictions.[16]

Before the Senate was established in St. Petersburg in 1711,
Russian laws were deposited in a variety of places, primarily in
Moscow. As mentioned earlier, one of Speranskii's most difficult tasks
was to determine from which state archives to take laws and decrees.
For the period between 1649 and 1711 Speranskii took laws from the
Estate Archives, the Archives of Ancient Acts and the Archives of the
College of Foreign Affairs in Moscow. After 1711, laws and decrees
came from a variety of different sources. They included the Archives
of the Holy Synod, of the War College, of the Naval Department and
those of many other ministries and their departments.[17]

However, Speranskii and the Second Section found that the
Commission on Laws under Alexander I had been through many of
these archives reviewing laws. Speranskii reported an extraordinary
number of laws removed by this earlier commission. However, all of
these laws were not accepted into this earlier group's major publication,
the *Systematic Survey* of 1821. It did, though, provide Speranskii with
a firm foundation for his work. For example, Speranskii noted that
from the Archives of the Senate in Moscow more than 23,000 laws
were removed by the earlier commission. However, from the numerous
other Moscow archives only 445 laws were considered. From the Senate
Archives in St. Petersburg over 20,000 laws were removed. And lastly,
nearly 9,000 laws were taken from the War College. Overall,
Alexander's commission removed over 53,000 laws and decrees from
only a few sources.[18] With the previous commissions' work as a solid
foundation, Speranskii made the physical arrangement of the
PSZ uniform, rational, and easy to use.

Speranskii outlined in his Preface ten general principles that
each law had to fulfill before inclusion into the *PSZ*. Even though all
of the laws came from the monarch, Speranskii noted the different
kinds of laws that were being considered. They included "statutes,
constitutions, instructions, patents, treatises, and decrees."[19] The first
guideline was that every law in the *PSZ* must the copied word for
word from the original. If the original included two languages, then

the foreign words must be translated into Russian for inclusion. The second principle referred to treatises, manifestoes, and patents with foreign powers. The treatises and other documents included began with Peter the Great's reign and only were relevant for "Great, White, and Small Russia."[20]

The third principle was to assign a number preceding the law in the collection. For example, the first entry was the *Ulozhenie* of 1649 so the number one (1) preceded this law. The fourth principle required that when available, the source of the law should be stated immediately after the number. The fifth and sixth principles required the date and place of issuance, if available, to follow the source. The seventh principle confronted the confusing issue of dates themselves. Many laws were issued on one date and not presented to the public until later, if at all. Speranskii determined that it was necessary to note the earliest date possible. Most of the discrepancies came from the War College for security reasons. Many decrees were not made public until later, so occasionally the exact date of the original was difficult to determine.[21]

The ninth and tenth principles maintained the idea of dividing volumes chronologically. The number of entries in each volume varied, but an effort was made to keep reigns included in a specific set of volumes. These were the principles upon which Speranskii based the physical appearance and publication of the *PSZ*.[22]

Such a collection would be difficult to use if it were not for the extensive index that followed. The *PSZ* was indexed in two ways. First, a chronological index provided the number and title of the law. The second index was an alphabetical one. Laws in this index were referred to in two ways. A key word was selected as the identifier from the title. This was a difficult task. All laws did not necessarily have a dominant or key word, or just one key word. It was for the members of the Second Section to determine what the key word would be. This produced many inconsistencies. For a researcher or jurist, the key word might be different from that of the Second Section member who indexed it in 1830. Without any standard way to index by key word, the alphabetical index was difficult to use. Following the key word would be the full title, volume number and law number.[23]

Two last volumes were also produced as additions to the *PSZ*. The first of these volumes contains statues and tariffs. Since these were important to the running of the Russian Empire, a special volume was produced to provide easy reference. The second volume is a collection of drawings and illustrations. When many of the laws were promulgated, drawings and illustrations were often included. This volume included the illustrations with proper citations of volume and law number.[24] With this organization of the *PSZ,* the Second Section members were expected to incorporate previous efforts and the newly discovered laws into this new collection.

Once the groundwork of the *PSZ* was thus laid, who did the work in the archives and how was it done? To document the daily activities of the Second Section from 1826 to 1830 would be tedious. However, to discuss how the work was carried out from one brief period will show how organized and, the times, disorganized it was.

Even though Speranskii stated that the work on the *PSZ* began in 1826 and ended in 1830, the majority of the work on this massive collection was completed by the end of 1828. At this time the work on the *SZ* began. The following discussion will focus on April and May 1826. The Second Section had several levels with Balug'ianskii and Speranskii at the top. Balug'ianskii was the official head, but his work on the *PSZ* was minimal. Speranskii, while holding no official title in the Second Section, did the majority of the organizational and editorial work. The next level of officials consisted of senior members. These members were Kunitsyn, Zimmerman, Korf, Arsenev, and Klokov. As noted earlier, each of these senior members were assigned a certain field of law to review.

Kunitsyn, who was the head of the senior members, was assigned to evaluate imperial laws for inclusion in the P*SZ*. He had the difficult task of reviewing laws in previous collections that concerned the imperial family. Being a trained jurist, he was well-prepared for this work, but in the end, Nicholas I censored many of the most sensitive laws related to the imperial family. Archival records show that Kunitsyn's daily tasks consisted of reviewing numerous laws. For instance, on April 26, 1826, he reviewed all laws concerning the imperial family between 1649 and 1696. Obviously, he did not complete this task alone. He assigned different sections to several assistants. If the first day's work seemed extraordinary, the rest of the following week certainly was more demanding. Between April 29, and May 4, 1826, archival records show that Kunitsyn reviewed all laws concerning the imperial family between 1696 and 1774. Even with the help of several assistants, Kunitsyn's and the other senior members' workloads were extraordinary.[25]

Even though Kunitsyn seemed to have the largest work load, the other senior members were expected to review large lists of laws quickly as well. In this same period, Korf was require to review state laws from three periods: 1725 to 1743, 1762 to 1774, and 1813 to 1823. Klokov reviewed personal laws covering the periods 1737 to 1763, 1743 to 1752, and 1752 to 1761. Lastly, Arsenev was assigned to review commercial laws from four periods including 1752 to 1762, 1725 to 1736, 1762 to 1779, and 1779 to 180.[27] All of this work was assigned to be completed in the last week of April and first week of May 1826. Such a work load only supported the notion held by many historians, like Marc Raeff, that Speranskii drove the Second Section very hard.[27]

The direction of the assistants was steered by Balug'ianskii. At any given time during the work on the *PSZ*, there were about twenty assistants in the Second Section these assistants had varied backgrounds and educations. Some were young seminary students who had been sent abroad for legal training in Prussia (as will be discussed in the following chapter) while others were career bureaucrats, many with strong Baltic German connections. All members of the Second Section met weekly to report their progress to Speranskii and Balug'ianskii and to receive further assignments. In addition, all members were sworn "to serve the emperor and take no act that would go against the general good of Russia and the crown."[28] With this loyalty pledge and other rationalizations of the project discussed earlier, it seemed unlikely that a truly complete collection would be compiled.

As for the work of the assistants, it differed somewhat from that of the senior members. Since most of the assistants did not have specialized legal training, most of their tasks were assigned chronologically rather than topically. At times, though, one senior member might work very closely with a particular assistant for an extended period on one project, but generally the duties were strictly chronological and rotated often. Also, the weekly meetings frequently did not give the name of the assistants when progress reports were given to Balug'ianskii. For example, in May 1826, Korf was reviewing the *Ulozhenie* of 1649 to find an appropriate version for inclusion in the *PSZ*. This was a lengthy project, but the identity of his assistant was never revealed in the weekly reports.[29] At the same time however, as Klokov reviewed personal laws, his assistants were referred to by name as Martinov and Kapir. They analyzed sections on personal law in the *Ulozhenie* of 1649 for inclusion in the *PSZ*.[30]

Another assignment delegated to the assistants was to get a total count of the number of laws that were to be included. In early May 1826 two counts appeared. The first was compiled by an anonymous assistant. His first count revealed that there were 22,020 laws from the *Ulozhenie* of 1649 to December 12, 1835 inclusive. A second count carried out by an assistant only referred to as Khavskii revealed 22,054, but his count ended on December 31, 1825. It would be safe to assume that these counts were identical, and the discrepancy came from laws in the last days of 1825. As noted earlier, Speranskii eventually changed the conclusion date to December 12, 1825 (the day Nicholas I took the throne). Nonetheless, this initial count fell well short of the final total of 30,920 in 1830. The Second Section reached this initial number (22,020) by simply reviewing the collections assembled by the previous legislative commissions of the eighteenth and early nineteenth centuries. So, only about 8,900 additional entries were added by the Second Section to the body of laws present in several collections published by previous commissions.[31] However, the Second Section tried to review all of the laws in previous collections before acceptance into the *PSZ*.

The lists of laws from prior commissions were organized chronologically and numbered. The assistants were then assigned certain numbers from certain periods to review. There did not seem to be a logical division of this labor. For instance, between April 25, and May 5, 1826, the assistants were assigned to review over 6,800 laws from 1649 to 1736. The three assistants referred to as Maier, Krug and Henning divided the work, but it followed neither topical nor chronological order. For example, Maier reviewed the laws numbered one through 114 from 1649 to 1651. Krug analyzed the laws numbered

115 to 771 from 1652 to 1674. But then Maier had another section from 1675 to 1676 and laws numbered 772 to 898. Following this Krug and Henning reviewed laws numbered 898 to 1397 from the years from 1677 to 1683. This raised the question of who reviewed which law. This alternating pattern would continue through law number 6,810 in 1736, without an explanation of the rationale.[32]

After 1736, this trend continued with some alterations. Other assistants became involved and Maier was no longer mentioned. Besides Krug and Henning, there were six other assistants added to review to work. The majority of the most important work fell upon assistants referred to as Mertz, Khavskii, and Terentev. These three reviewed laws that covered most of Catherine II's reign, including those during the Legislative Commission of 1767-1768. The of reviewing old lists of laws dominated the early work of the assistants, but the accumulation of new laws would soon start.[33]

Once the work of reviewing the previous lists concluded, the members of the Second Section then investigated the archives for additional laws. By the end of May 1826, much of the work of collecting laws from the archives was assigned to assistants Mertz, Khavskii, and Terentev. One of the first things they discovered in several of the archives was that there were several lists and registries that often duplicated the identification of laws leaving an accurate count of laws difficult to determine. In just a few weeks of investigation, these assistants also discovered more than 400 additional laws that needed to be reviewed for inclusion from the reigns of Peter I, Catherine I, and Elizabeth.[34] Khavskii compiled a complete list of their recent discoveries into three books and while laws were being reviewed by assistants and senior members when other members found another 297 laws for review from Peter I's era and 41 from the reign of Empress Anna. In the end, Speranskii recorded that for the periods 1649 through 1674 and 1715 through 1725, the earlier lists were fairly complete and few new laws were added.[35] This rationalization seems odd considering Speranskii reviewed all of the lists and knew of the new discoveries which numbered more than 700 new entries.

While the assistants toiled away in the archives reviewing lists and searching for additional laws, the senior members spent much of their time reviewing the work of the assistants and developing historical surveys for each of their respective sections. Kunitsyn, Korf, and Arsenev drafted historical surveys of Russian law and theoretical works on Russian law. Kunitsyn's historical work was supposed to appear in the *PSZ* after the section ending in 1714. However, Speranskii later decided that the *PSZ* would only be a list and full text of laws without historical or theoretical writings. For Korf and Arsenev, their work was more theoretical and intended for the *SZ*, but their work also did not appear in the digest.[36]

By the summer of 1826 Nicholas I was concerned about the progress of the work of the Second Section. He wanted the historical collection to be completed as quickly as possible so they could move on the compile the *SZ*. He wanted an active code of laws to maintain a firm control in Russia. The emperor sent a letter to Speranskii, Balug'ianskii, and the Second Section instructing them to shift several assistants away from the historical collection to work on current legal matters. Nicholas I also proposed a method of division for the historical collection. He did not understand the need to divide the *PSZ* by reign, so he divided it into four periods. The first was the *Ulozhenie* of 1649. The second was from 1649 to 1714. The third was from 1714 to 1762 and the last was from 1762 to 1825. He did this to simplify and speed the work of the Second Section.[37] Nicholas and Speranskii agreed on the necessity to complete the *PSZ* quickly, but they differed on the collection's scope and arrangement. Speranskii initially wanted a complete collection while Nicholas viewed this exercise as a survey of some of the past laws which would lead to a strong active code.

By early 1827 it was clear that the Second Section was only working in the Senate archives in St. Petersburg and reviewing lists sent from other archives primarily in Moscow. Since the overall list of laws was generally complete, the assistants spent much of their time comparing versions of laws held both in archives in St. Petersburg and Moscow. This was a particularly difficult task. What versions of laws were the assistants to submit for the collection? Often the earliest version was accepted, but on several occasions an amalgamation of several different versions was constructed by an assistant.[38] Such review and reconstruction created inconsistencies in the law.

Additionally, the senior members had moved on the other tasks by 1827. Much of the work on the *PSZ* had become clerical in nature so the focus shifted to the *SZ*. Kunitsyn began to examine laws concerning three broad areas including acquisitions, division of general laws, and spiritual testaments. Arsenev continued his work on commercial law for the *SZ*. Korf, however, continued to supervise the revision of laws for inclusion in the *PSZ* until its publication was complete in 1830. Lastly, Klokov, who was a minor figure in this work on the *PSZ*, was assigned the task of looking at nine different areas related to the *SZ*. They included the imperial family, people removed by monarchs, specific departments, treasury, noble society, common society, churches and monasteries, rural society, and foreign colony settlements.[39]

From the earlier discussion it might seem that the majority of the work was done by the assistants and senior members, while Speranskii and Balug'ianskii remained idle. The work of Speranskii and Balug'ianskii, however, was a supervisory one. They constantly reviewed the work of all members of the Second Section and made work assignments on a weekly basis. During this work, they were also preparing for the compilation of the *SZ*. As noted earlier, Speranskii went to Moscow at least once during this work to review lists from several archives. Part of the difficulty the Second Section encountered was that the people in the archives in Moscow especially, but also in St. Petersburg, who compiled the archival lists knew little of the law or of the purpose of this project. Speranskii sent several letters with the lists of laws to Balug'ianskii. In these letters he admonished the director of the Second Section to be as thorough as possible in the reviewing of this material from Moscow. Speranskii reported that most of the material from the period 1649 through 1711 was found in the Senate archives in St. Petersburg and Moscow.[40] By late 1827, Speranskii and Balug'ianskii were frustrated by the lack of trained jurists in the Second Section. They needed more and better trained assistants to carry out the work of the Second Section. Speranskii was concerned about the nature of an active code of law in Russia with so few trained to use it properly.

For Speranskii, the purpose of the *SZ* was to provide Russia with a clear and efficient reference work of active laws for jurists and judges to use as a guide to the *PSZ*. Speranskii believed there were two kinds of legal bonds upon which the structure and organization of the *SZ* should be based. He thought there were political or state obligations and civil obligations. The difference in the development of state laws compared to civil laws was dramatic. The state law, those issued by the monarch, were numerous and well-defined throughout the eighteenth and early nineteenth centuries. However, the civil laws which included police, criminal, and property laws were extremely underdeveloped in Russia.[41]

Speranskii outlined the organization of the *SZ* in introductory material to the collection. He made a solid connection between the *SZ* and the earlier *PSZ*. Speranskii stated that

> *All decrees and resolutions in the space of 176 years still in force from all categories, in one collection, given in a systematic form in order that they were presented in one whole, one book that would be of one understanding... without repetition and contradiction.*[42]

Unlike the *PSZ*, though, the *SZ* was organized topically rather than chronologically. Speranskii and others in the Second Section realized that Russian law was quite disorganized and contained few general principles upon which laws were based. Speranskii wanted to modernize Russian law along European lines so he looked to several different European nations for legal models.

However, as the work on the *SZ* began in 1828, several different visions about the purpose and scope of this digest emerged. Speranskii explained that his first idea had two parts. Initially, it was important to justify the usefulness of the new digest of laws. Critics argued that the *Ulozhenie* of 1649 certainly had served as an adequate law code and there was no reason to change at this point. Speranskii argued that "the ordering and distribution of new laws according to the articles of the *Ulozhenie* [of 1649], served as the explanation and reasoning"[43] for the issuance of a new active code of laws for Russia. Speranskii asserted that the classification of laws put forth in the *Ulozhenie* of 1649 would not be altered, rather the digest would just be an update of more current laws.

The second part of Speranskii's first vision explained how the Second Section should include all of the relevant new laws and even replace old ones from the *Ulozhenie* with more recent laws. This seems to contradict the first idea which sought to preserve certain elements of the *Ulozhenie*. Yet, Speranskii felt that the original thirteen sections or chapters of the earlier law code should be followed for the new one.[44] Unfortunately, the state of law in Russia in the early nineteenth century was significantly different from 1649 and many of the older categories did not fit the modern needs. Speranskii would have to eventually abandon the older categories as he incorporated modern legal concepts and categories.

Speranskii's second vision for this *SZ* addressed exactly which laws would be included in the active code. He wanted all of the older laws that had been replaced by more current legislation to be removed altogether. He wanted only the most current law on any given issue to be considered the active legislation to eliminate the possibility of contradiction or duplication.[45] His third and fourth ideas dealt with the particularly important issues of the integrity of the wording of laws and reducing the size of the entries. Speranskii was concerned about how laws in the *SZ*, which were extracted from larger and numerous legal texts, would retain their meaning and importance. According to historian P.M. Maikov, Speranskii wanted

The integrity of the word of law, extractions from articles of the Digest should be taken primarily from texts and observations so that the articles which were seized from one active decree or resolution set forth the same words to stand in the text without all of their changes.[46]

Additionally, Speranskii was concerned about the length of the entry of each law. Since the *SZ* was intended to be a reference work, brevity was necessary. He did not want the entries to be so long that they were not understandable or useful to jurists or judges. Speranskii was caught in the delicate situation of needing to reduce the length of the entries while trying to retain their textual integrity. In the end, Speranskii often altered many laws to make them fit into certain categories.

Speranskii then outlined the four key questions facing the Second Section as they compiled the *SZ*. He first wanted the Second Section "To define with precision the essence of the work and its main principles."[47] Speranskii believed that this *SZ* was particularly important because not only was it a collection of active laws, but because of many of the additions and innovations in the digest it became a source of law itself. Here it was clear that Speranskii still desired an abstract code of law, an idea rejected by Nicholas I in 1826. The other three elements for the work on the *SZ* were more bureaucratic in nature. First Speranskii wanted members of the Second Section "to compose a general plan for the division of the laws."[48] The *PSZ* was arranged chronologically when it was published in 1830, but as noted earlier, the work was carried out by members of the Second Section topically. In the *SZ*, there were eight books of law in fifteen volumes. The work of the members of the Second Section was conducted according to these eight books or areas of law. The last two principles related to the actual work itself. Speranskii wanted the Second Section to carry out preparatory work and then "establish a definitive work."[49]

Once the work on the *SZ* had been completed in 1833, Speranskii issued a statement which outlined the application of the articles of the *SZ*. Speranskii stated that

in all of these occurrences, where laws were placed in the code from their notes, they were pointed out in the Table of Contents from January 1, 1835 on... they were to issue instructions and references to the articles in the Digest, in the proper manner.[50]

Speranskii followed this general statement with several much more specific guidelines that needed to be followed as laws were being considered for inclusion in the *SZ*.

The first guideline each entry had to meet in order to be included in the *SZ* was that it needed to be identified in three ways. First, the volume number was crucial. With the *SZ* being a reference work, the omission of the volume number of the *PSZ* would make it nearly impossible to find the appropriate entry. The second identifier was the title of the law or decree. Often judges, jurist or researchers would only know the title of the law, but little else so this system helped locate those laws. The last element was the number of the law. Each law was assigned a number in the chronological collection. Since the *SZ* was organized topically, it was important for the law number from the *PSZ* to appear in the new digest. An additional way to find the appropriate reference was using the alphabetical index. Problems would occasionally occur with this index because there were not any standardized alphabetical procedures.[51] To help make this alphabetical index more useful, Speranskii directed the Second Section to use only abbreviations in the *SZ* that were already present in the *PSZ*. Speranskii hoped this would reduce confusion, introduce a measure of standardization between the collections, and make them both more useful. Yet, confusion over the alphabetical index persisted.[52]

The third guideline Speranskii put forth for the *SZ* was how to cite the law properly in the digest. He felt that it was important in all cases to cite the volume number, title and law number of the entry. However, there were times when there were notes that gave the source that could serve as the identifier. When citing passages in the same text from the same volume, it was only necessary to note the page number and the year of the law. In the cases where notes were used as the references, Speranskii wondered how to refer to these laws since there was an element of confusion. Even though these laws were not issued by the monarch, Speranskii decided that they were important and could be retained as "founding decisions."[53]

The fourth principle Speranskii outlined for the *SZ* was concerned with the sequel or next edition of the this collection. The first series was issued in 1833 and took effect in 1835, but Speranskii's plan laid out originally was for there to be a sequel or supplement to the *SZ* every year so the digest would be an accurate digest of the laws currently in force. Speranskii wanted to maintain the integrity of the laws themselves as well, so he instructed members of the Second Section to incorporate the newest laws without variation of language.[54] Speranskii also believed that this update should be an annual yearbook. When using laws from preceding digests they should be organized under similar themes according to the original eight books of law in the *SZ*. When alterations had to be made to laws, Speranskii wanted these changes to be noted as these articles were placed into the proper book according to their specific area of law.[55] However, there were only three sequels or updated to the *SZ* issued before the end of the empire in 1917.

In the cases of state affairs, Speranskii was concerned about how these laws were implemented. Since court cases constantly used current and past laws as the basis for current decisions, Speranskii felt that some of these cases might interpret laws in such a way that would alter the fundamental meaning of the law and thus create a new legal norm for Russia. Speranskii resolved the dilemma by deciding that after January 1, 1835 all court decisions had to be compared to the appropriate law for accuracy. If there were no law that corresponded, then the court decisions could be added in one of the updates to the *SZ*.[56] However, it is unclear whether or not Nicholas agreed with giving judges such broad interpretive powers. Speranskii's idea left judges and jurists with the power to alter Russian legal norms and in essence issue laws themselves.

Despite all of these guidelines, Speranskii outlined several exceptions. First, all resolutions or laws issued after January 1, 1834 were to be entered in the first of the sequels to the *SZ*. The second exception was that "all local law codes were not to be included in the digest."[57] Local law codes from provincial areas of the Russian empire created a sensitive problem for Speranskii and the Second Section. In order to rationalize and simplify the digest, Speranskii simply omitted the local law codes from the *SZ*.[58] The last exceptions were concerning those areas of government and society that were not to be included in the *SZ*. It is clear that these exceptions which concerned the Ministry of Public Enlightenment, state inspectors and accounting, statutes from foreign governments, and postal regulations, were Speranskii's further attempts to keep the digest simple and efficient. He tried to eliminate those areas of law that did not appear essential and created confusion.[59]

It was under these guidelines that Speranskii wanted the *SZ* to be compiled. Obviously, this project was more complicated than the work on the *PSZ* had been. The complexities of law and legal interpretation were now in play. The work on the *PSZ* had been quite bureaucratic and tedious. The organization of the *SZ* was Speranskii's attempt to make the digest more efficient, rational and usable.

Speranskii reported that the work on the *PSZ*, or the "historical collection" was completed by January 24, 1828.[60] Archival records show that Speranskii directed the senior members of the Second Section and their assistants to begin work on the *SZ* the following day, January 25, 1828. Balug'ianskii and Speranskii assigned Alexander Kunitsyn, Modest A. Korf, Dmitri Klokov and Dmitri Plisov as the senior members for this work. The primary assistants were referred to as Keller, Zamiatnin, Illichevskii, and Eristov.[61]

Each senior member was responsible for the compilation of one section of laws concerning criminal law and the police. Kunitsyn was assigned criminal law, so his task was to review the *PSZ* to find the most current laws in force on a variety of criminal topics. Klokov was assigned one section on the police while Korf and Plisov were assigned police laws on delinquency. The assistants were divided evenly among these difficult sections. Each was assigned a section that they could complete quickly.[62]

Throughout the spring of 1828, the work was mainly carried out by the senior members. Speranskii took a special interest in this work, and it was apparent that he was concerned with the overall digest and how the laws related to one another. It is clear that many of the laws were contradictory. Kunitsyn focused much of his work on the second book of the *SZ*. He reviewed criminal laws for inclusion with the help of his assistant, Keller. They were particularly concerned about the clarity of laws, removing contradictions, and making sure that all types of criminality were covered by these laws.[63] Speranskii and Balug'ianskii, though, knew of the importance of developing an appeals system so Kunitsyn was also assigned the task of developing a Court of Appeals for Russia.[64] Kunitsyn seemed to have received the most challenging and important tasks among the senior members of the Second Section. This reliance on Kunitsyn was because of his expertise as a jurist and his long-time friendship with Balug'ianskii.

By 1829, Kunitsyn's work shifted to reviewing police laws while Korf was examining a wide range of civil laws. For a time, Kunitsyn took over the more bureaucratic duties once carried out by Balug'ianskii, while the director and Speranskii wrestled with how to organize and make references to laws.[65] Plisov also became more prominent in his legal investigations. He analyzed the laws that related to church and spiritual matters because the laws in this area were quite confused. From the late seventeenth century to the early nineteenth century, the legal status of the church changed significantly.[66] Plisov researched legal precedents to try and define the current condition, but was not terribly successful.[67] Additionally, Plisov was assigned to review all laws related to universities and education, in general, in

Russia. Klokov, another of the senior members, was assigned to review all laws concerning forestry, salt, and the mining of money. While these areas might seem minor compared to the areas of civil, criminal, and state law, they were actually crucial topics, especially for provincial areas.[68]

Even though the work of the senior members was constantly shifting, a few general principles for work assignments existed. For Kunitsyn, review of police laws, civil laws, and criminal laws consistently occupied his time. At the same time, he also would occasionally review laws concerning such obscure topics as the theatre. Plisov also reviewed sections of the police, civil, and criminal codes. Yet, he was responsible for all laws concerning churches and medicine as well for the *SZ*.[69] Korf's chief duty was to review civil law for inclusion in the *SZ*. As noted earlier, this section was one of the most difficult and controversial. He also reviewed several sections of state laws as well as laws concerning factory practices. Klokov's assignment usually concerned laws on rural areas, land, and peasantry. Several other assistants had narrow of law assigned to them as well. As 1829 ended, so did the work on the *SZ*.[70]

As the work on the *SZ* continued, archival records show periodically that from late 1828 to 1830, numerous volumes of the *PSZ* were being published by the Second Section. A typical entry from Balug'ianskii would note the end date for the current volume being published. For example, on May 1, 1829, Balug'ianskii reported that the fourteenth volume of the *PSZ* was published and ended with the death of Catherine II in 1769. These entries occasionally mentioned the length of the volumes, the number of laws included in the volume, and the number of copies to be printed.[71]

Kunitsyn and Korf were in charge of reviewing all of the laws to be introduced in the *SZ*. They were making certain that the wording of the laws was clear enough to find the full text of the law in the *PSZ*.[72] However, in 1830, the Second Section experienced some dramatic changes. First, the majority of the *PSZ* was published in this year and it was officially issued. It is clear that in 1830 most of the energy was directed to finishing the publishing of the *PSZ*. By the middle of 1830, the work on the *SZ* had ended and the focus was shifted to working on provincial law; a task for which several new members had been added.[73] Additionally, work also began on the second series of the *PSZ*. Speranskii's idea was to update this historical collection every year. So, as the first series was being published issued in 1830, the Second Section began the work of collecting laws between December 12, 1825 and January 1, 1830 for the beginning of the second series of the *PSZ*.[74]

An initial count of published laws revealed that between the death of Alexander I in 1825 and 1830, thousands of laws had been issued. It also revealed that the source of Russian law was still varied. In this five year period there were nearly 1,600 laws issued by Nicholas I or in his name. But further research revealed that another 1,600 laws were issued from twenty different departments of the government. The largest issuers of laws was the Council of Ministers with more than 500 credited the them. Two others that exceeded 150 laws each were the Ministry of War and the Ministry of the Navy.[75]

The integrity of the wording of the entries in the *SZ* was also a crucial question. In numerous cases, especially concerning civil law, there were inconsistencies and discrepancies in Russian law. Speranskii and other senior members took it upon themselves to reorganize some of the more confusing areas. Raeff asserts that "By citing out of context, by running together several acts, summarizing them, and providing connecting paragraphs, Speransky actually interpreted the laws and sometimes even created new norms and concepts."[76] Raeff maintains that the *SZ* was now not simply a digest of the current laws, but rather it was developing into some sort of code of laws.

Most of Speranskii's work was on law concerned European Russia while the role of law in the provincial areas remained ambiguous. This is a subject that is peripheral to this study, but very important in Russian legal development. The Second Section worked for several years collecting laws from all over the empire. Speranskii recognized that the Russian Empire was multinational with dozens of languages and many distinct concepts of legal norms. The tensions between the Russian government and several of its peripheral territories, especially the Baltic areas and Western provinces, made the issuance of the *SZ* a particularly sensitive issue for the government.[77] Ideally, the *SZ* was to be the active code of law for the empire, but political tensions required that Speranskii recognize the legal norms of some provincial areas.

The Second Section collected thousands of laws from all over the empire, but only one separate code was issued at this time and that was for the Baltic areas. However, this code was severely restricted by Speranskii's narrow understanding of the Baltic legal norms and Nicholas I's refusal to allow any real measure of legal autonomy.[78] Unfortunately there have been few detailed studies of these provincial codes. One section of the *SZ* that has been studied by scholars, however, is the area concerning civil law. M.M. Vinaver's study from the late nineteenth century provides a good survey of this topic.[79]

The tenth volume of the *SZ* consisted of civil laws. It was probably one of the most controversial sections of this digest. Speranskii especially wanted one of the eight books to deal with civil law. He felt that for legal progress along European lines, Russia had to have well-developed civil laws. However, Speranskii found that Russia's legal heritage was lacking any real depth in the area of civil law. So, as the P*SZ* was being compiled, Speranskii realized this deficiency and continued to advocate a separate book on civil law for the *SZ*.[80] Theoretically, the *SZ* was reference book for the *PSZ*. As mentioned before, a jurist or judge could use the *SZ* to find a summary or description of the law and its location in the *PSZ*. However, for civil laws, as Vinaver pointed out, Speranskii borrowed heavily from two main sources. First, he used his own earlier legal ideas and writings as a source of civil law. He especially referred to his "Vvedenie k ulozheniu gosudarstvennikh zakonov" (more commonly known as the "Plan of 1809").[81] This very plan had been one of the factors that led to his exile in 1812. Vinaver notes how Speranskii had changed his legal thinking from 1812 to 1826. Speranskii had once relied on foreign laws for formulation of abstract legal essays like his "Plan of 1809," but now he had matured intellectually and politically and utilized an historical approach to codification.[82] As Raeff notes, though, Speranskii was only supposed to refer to laws previously issued, and his "Plan of 1809" was never enacted.[83]

The second source of civil law of the *SZ* was foreign legal models. The three examples Vinaver uses in his study were French, Roman, and German. Vinaver asserts that undoubtedly the French influence was the greatest. Of course this is only reinforced by Speranskii's reliance upon his own "Plan of 1809" which was heavily influenced by and criticized for its reliance upon the French *Code Napoleon* of 1800.[84] Ever though Roman and German law were not borrowed from as heavily by Speranskii, Vinaver chronicles dozens of laws in the tenth volume (civil law) of the *SZ* that came from both of these legal traditions.

In the end, civil law in Russia was incomplete. Speranskii took steps to modernize or Europeanize Russian civil law. Vinaver clearly outlines dozens of laws in the *SZ* that came directly from foreign sources, especially French. His conclusion is that Speranskii's liberal leaning was clearly evident in his reliance upon French law. While Raeff agrees that Speranskii used foreign legal models heavily, he maintains it was only for bureaucratic rationalization of Russian law. He did not see Speranskii's later legal efforts as particularly liberal, but purely bureaucratic efforts to create a more efficient legal system for a more efficient and rational government in Russia.[85]

According to historian Richard C. Wortman, Speranskii's adoption of the historical approach to jurisprudence pleased Nicholas because the emperor felt that this approach "banished the notion that law had to conform to universal natural norms, and consecrating the statutes issued by the autocrat, exempted them from outside judgment."[86] Nicholas' fear of an abstract legal code was apparent as he did not want to leave Russian law open to interpretation. While he appeared to trust Balug'ianskii and Speranskii, he continued to take an active role at ever stage of this codification process.[87]

Archival and manuscript investigations tend to support Raeff's assertion. In Speranskii's notes, essays, government reports, and letters rarely did he refer to his initial plan for creating a new abstract law code. Once Nicholas I had rejected the abstract code, Speranskii never mentioned it again. His task was one of rationalization as it had been in his reforms of the Siberian administration a decade earlier. Speranskii realized, though, that the task of searching for foreign legal models and domestic legal sources for a basis of Russian civil law would require a well-trained group of jurists. The next section shows the importance of the Second Section members continuing their legal studies once they returned to Russia.

NOTES:

[1] Mikhail M. Speranskii, "Predislovie k *Polnoe Sobranie Zakonov,"* 1830, RGIA, F. 1251: Bumagi M.M. Speranskago, op. 1, d. 132, 11. 1-10.

[2] Speranskii, "Predislovie," 1830, RGIA, F. 1251: Bumagi M.M. Speranskago, op. 1, d. 132, 11. 7-11; "Predislovie," *PSZ* vi-vii; A.E. Nolde, *Ocherki istorii kodifikatsii mestnykh grazhdanskikh zakonov pri grafa Speranskom* (St. Petersburg, 1906), I, 31-58.

[3] Speranskii, "Predislovie," 1830, RGIA, F. 1251: Bumagi M.M. Speranskago, op. 1, d. 132, 11. 8-12; "Predislovie," *PSZ*, ix-x.

[4] Speranskii, "Predislovie," 1830, RGIA, F. 1251: Bumagi M.M. Speranskago, op. 1, d. 132, 11. 8-12; "Predislovie," *PSZ*, xi; P.M. Maikov, *Vtoroe otdelenie sobstvennoi ego imperatorskago velichestva kantseliarii, 1826-1882* (St. Petersburg, 1906), 138-55.

[5] Raeff, *Michael Speransky,* 323-35; Maikov, *Vtoroe,* 138-52.

[6] A. Filippov, "K voprosu o sostave pervogo Polnogo Sobraniia Zakonov Rossiiskoi Imperii," *Otchet Imperatorskogo Moskovskogo Universiteta za 1915 g* (Moscow, 1916), I, 78-79; Raeff, *Michael Speransky,* 326-28. Codification efforts in the Western provinces are discussed in A.E. Nolde, *Ocherki istorii kodifikatsii mestnykh grazhdanskikh zakonov pri grafa Speranskom* (St. Petersburg, 1906).

[7] G. Telberg, "Uchastie Imperatora Nikolaia I v kodifikatsionnoi rabote ego tsarstvovanniia," *Zhurnal Ministerstva Iustitsii* 22 : 1 (January 1916): 233-44.

[8] Speranskii, "Predislovie," 1830, RGIA, F.1251: Bumagi M.M. Speranskago, op. 1, d. 132, 11. 11-21; Raeff, *Michael Speransky,* 328-30.

[9] Speranskii, "Predislovie," 1830, RGIA, F. 1251: Bumagi M.M. Speranskago, op. 1, d. 132, 11. 15-21; Raeff, *Michael Speransky,* 328; Filippov, "K voprosu," 25-30; "Predislovie," *PSZ*, vi-xviii; A. Fateev,

"K istorii i teorii kodifikatsii – stoletie Polnogo Sobraniia Zakonov," *Russkii Narodnyi universitet v Prage – Nauchnye Trudy* IV (1931) 11-12, 105-113; Richard Hellie, trans. and ed., *The Muscovite Law Code (Ulozhenie) of 1649* (Irvine, CA: Charles Schlacks Jr., Publishers, 1988-89), I, xx-xxvii.

[10] "Memorii o trudakh chinovnikom IIgo otdelenie sobstvennoi ego imperatorskago velichestva kantseliarii," February 5, 1827, RGIA, F. 1251: Bumagi M.M. Speranskago, op. 1, d. 86a, 1. 12; Filippov, "K voprosu," 110-30; Raeff, *Michael Speransky*, 330. See Nolde, *Ocherki istorii kodifikatsii* for a discussion of Baltic Law.

[11] "Perepiska Speranskago s rasnumi litsami i raportu emu Balug'ianskogo," August 27, 1826, RGIA, F. 1251: Bumagi M.M. Speranskago, op. 1, d. 83, 11. 8-9.

[12] "Memorii o trudakh chinovnikom IIgo otdeleniia sobstvennoi ego Imperatorskago velichestva kantseliarii zanumaushchikhsia svobami," April 24, 1836, RGIA, F. 1251: Bumagi M.M. Speranskago, op. 1, d. 86, 11. 2-3.

[13] Ibid.

[14] "Predislovie," *PSZ*, xviii; Speranskii, "Predislovie," 1830, RGIA, F. 1251: Bumagi M.M. Speranskago, op. 1, d. 132, 11. 15-17.

[15] "Predislovie," *PSZ*, xviii-xix; Speranskii, "Predislovie," 1830, RGIA, F. 1251: Bumagi M.M. Speranskago, op. 1, d. 132, 11. 21-30.

[16] "Predislovie," *PSZ*, xix.

[17] Ibid., xix-xxi; Speranskii, "Predislovie," 1830, RGIA, F. 1251: Bumagi M.M. Speranskago, op. 1, d. 132, 11. 22-25.

[18] "Predislovie," *PSZ*, xxii-xxiv; Speranskii, "Predislovie," 1830, RGIA, F. 1251: Bumagi M.M. Speranskago, op. 1, d. 132, 11. 27-30.

[19] "Predislovie," *PSZ*, xxiv.

[20] Ibid., xxv.

21 Ibid., xxiv-xxvi; Raeff, *Michael Speransky*, 328-32.

22 "Predislovie," *PSZ*, xxvi; Speranskii, "Predislovie," 1830, RGIA, F. 1251: Bumagi M.M. Speranskago, op. 1, d. 132, 1. 30.

23 "Predislovie," *PSZ*, xxvii-xxviii.

24 Ibid., xxviii-xxix.

25 "Memorii o trudakh chinovnikom IIgo otdeleniia sobstvennoi ego imperatorskago velichestva kantseliarii zanimaushchikhsia svobami," May 12, 1826, RGIA, F. 1251: Bumagi M.M. Speranskii, op. 1, d. 86, 1. 19.

26 Ibid.

27 Raeff, *Michael Speransky,* 320-330.

28 "Memorii o trudakh chinovnikom IIgo otedleniia sobstvennoi ego imperatorskago velichestva kantseliarii zanimaushchikhsia svobami," April 27, 1826, RGIA, F. 1251: Bumagi M.M. Speranskago, op. 1, d. 86, 1. 4.

29 "Memorii o trudakh chinovnikom IIgo otedleniia sobstvennoi ego imperatorskago velichestva kantseliarii zanimaushchikhsia svobami," May 12, 1826, RGIA, F. 1251: Bumagi M.M. Speranskago, op. 1, d. 86, 1. 11.

30 Ibid.

31 Ibid., 12.

32 "Memorii o trudakh chinovnikom IIgo otedleniia sobstvennoi ego imperatorskago velichestva kantseliarii zanimaushchikhsia svobami," May 19, 1826, RGIA, F. 1251: Bumagi M.M. Speranskago, op. 1, d. 86, 1. 21.

33 Ibid., 23-24.

34 "Memorii o trudakh chinovnikom IIgo otedleniia sobstvennoi ego imperatorskago velichestva kantseliarii zanimaushchikhsia svobami,"

May 22, 1826, RGIA, F. 1251: Bumagi M.M. Speranskago, op. 1, d. 86, 11. 71-78.

[35] Ibid.

[36] "Memorii o trudakh chinovnikom IIgo otedleniia sobstvennoi ego imperatorskago velichestva kantseliarii zanimaushchikhsia svobami," June 9, 1826, RGIA, F. 1251: Bumagi M.M. Speranskago, op. 1, d. 86, 11. 83-88.

[37] "Memorii o trudakh chinovnikom IIgo otedleniia sobstvennoi ego imperatorskago velichestva kantseliarii zanimaushchikhsia svobami," May 22, 1826, RGIA, F. 1251: Bumagi M.M. Speranskago, op. 1, d. 86, 11. 69; G. Telberg, "Uchastie," 233-44.

[38] "Perepiska Speranskogo s rasnymi litsami i raportu emu Balug'ianskogo," July 1, 1826, RGIA, F. 1251: Bumagi M.M. Speranskago, op. 1, d. 83, 11. 1-3.

[39] "Memorii o trudakh chinovnikom IIgo otdelenie sobstvennoi ego imperatorskago velichestva kantseliarii." January 5, 1827, RGIA, F. 1251: Bumagi M.M. Speranskago, op 1, d. 86a, 11. 2-5.

[40] "Perepiska Speranskogo s rasnymi litsami i raportu emu Balug'ianskogo," July 1, 1826, RGIA, F. 1251: Bumagi M.M. Speranskogo, op. 1, d. 83, 1. 4.

[41] Mikhail M. Speranskii, *Precis des Notions historiques sur la formation du Corps des lois russes* (St. Petersburg, 1833), 116-17.

[42] Mikhail M. Speranskii, "Vvedenie k Svode Grazhdanskikh Zakonov," 1832, RGIA, F. 1251: Bumagi M.M. Speranskago, op. 1, d. 110, 11. 30-31.

[43] Mikhail M. Speranskii, *Obozrenie istoricheskikh svedenii o Svod Zakonov* (St. Petersburg, 1833), 47.

[44] Ibid., 47-48.

[45] P.M. Maikov, *Vtoroe otdelenie sobstvennoi ego imperatorskago velichestva kantseliarii, 1826-1882* (St. Petersburg, 1906) 169.

[46] Ibid., 169.

[47] Speranskii, *Obozrenie*, 68.

[48] Ibid.

[49] Ibid.

[50] "Podrobnoe nastavlenie o propodzhenii i utotreblenii statei Svoda v proizvodstve del," 1835, RGIA, F. 1251: Bumagi M.M. Speranskago, op. 1, d. 162, 11. 25-26.

[51] Ibid., 26.

[52] Ibid.

[53] Ibid., 27.

[54] Ibid., 28.

[55] Ibid.

[56] Ibid., 28-29.

[57] Ibid., 29.

[58] Ibid., 29.

[59] Ibid., 29-30.

[60] "Memorii o trudakh chinovnikom IIgo otdeleniia sobstvennoi ego imperatorskago velichestva kantseliarii," February 8, 1828, RGIA, F. 1251: Bumagi M.M. Speranskago, op. 1, d. 86b, 1. 2.

[61] Ibid., 3.

[62] Ibid., 3-4.

[63] "Memorii o trudakh chinovnikom IIgo otdeleniia sobstvennoi ego imperatorskago velichestva kantseliarii," March 7, 1828, RGIA, F. 1251: Bumagi M.M. Speranskago, op. 1, d. 86b, 11. 9-10.

64 "Memorii o trudakh chinovnikom IIgo otdeleniia sobstvennoi ego imperatorskago velichestva kantseliarii," April 14, 1828, RGIA, F. 1251: Bumagi M.M. Speranskago, op. 1, d. 86b, 1. 19.

65 "Memorii o trudakh chinovnikom IIgo otdeleniia sobstvennoi ego imperatorskago velichestva kantseliarii," September 11, 1829, RGIA, F. 1251: Bumagi M.M. Speranskago, op. 1, d. 86v, 11. 51-54.

66 For a complete discussion òf Peter the Great's church reform see James Cracraft, *The Church Reform of Peter the Great* (Stanford: Stanford University Press, 1971).

67 "Memorii o trudakh chinovnikom IIgo otdeleniia sobstvennoi ego imperatorskago velichestva kantseliarii," December 18, 1829, RGIA, F. 1251: Bumagi M.M. Speranskago, op. 1, d. 86v, 11. 80-81.

68 "O zaniatiiakh IIgo otdeleniia sobstvennoi ego imperatorskago velichestva kantseliarii," October 18, 1828, RGIA, F. 1251: Bumagi M.M. Speranskago, op. 1, d. 86b, 11. 74-76.

69 "Obshchii vid zaniatii chinovnikom II otdeleniia v 1829 godu," 1829, RGIA, F. 1251: Bumagi M.M. Speranskago, op. 1, d. 86b, 1. 45a.

70 Ibid., 45a-45b.

71 "Memorii o trudakh chinovnikom IIgo otdeleniia sobstvennoi ego imperatorskago velichestva kantseliarii," May 15, 1829, RGIA, F. 1251: Bumagi M.M. Speranskago, op. 1, d. 86v, 11. 24-26.

72 Ibid., 30-32.

73 "Memorii o trudakh chinovnikom IIgo otdeleniia sobstvennoi ego imperatorskago velichestva kantseliarii," February 12, 1830, RGIA, F. 1251: Bumagi M.M. Speranskago, op. 1, d. 86g, 11. 11-13.

74 "Otchet o zaniatiiakh IIgo otdeleniia vremia otsutstvaia ego vysokorevoskhoditelstva Mikhaila Mikhailovicha Speranskago ot Maia 17 po Sentiabria 15, 1830 goda," 1830, RGIA, F. 1251: Bumagi M.M. Speranskago, op. 1, d. 86g, 11. 33-35.

75 "Uzakonenii sobrannykh c 12go Dekabria 1825go 1 do Ianvaria 1830 goda vo IIgo otdeleniia sobstvennoi ego imperatorskago velichestva kantseliarii," 1830, RGIA, F. 1251: Bumagi M.M. Speranskago, op. 1, d. 86g, 11. 37-38.

76 Raeff, *Michael Speransky*, 335.

77 Maikov, *Vtoroe*, 170.

78 Raeff, *Michael Speransky*, 340-42; For a full discussion of local codes see A.E. Nolde, *Ocherki istorii kodifikatsii mestnykh grazhdanskikh zakonov pri grafe Speranskom* 2 vols. (St. Petersburg, 1906, 1914).

79 M.M. Vinaver, "K voprosu ob istochnikakh X toma Svoda Zakonov," *Zhurnal Ministerstva Iustitsii* (October 1895) : 1-68; (June 1897) : 87-102.

80 Vinaever, "K voprosu," (October 1895) : 1-20; Raeff, *Michael Speransky*, 335-40.

81 Mikhail M. Speranskii, "Vvedenie k ulozheniu gosudarstvennikh zakonov (1809g.)," in *Plan gosudarstvennikh preobrazovanniia grafa M.M. Speranskago* (Moscow, 1905), 1-120.

82 See Chapter 1 of this study for a discussion of Speranskii's legal thought.

83 Vinaver, "K voprosu," 20-28; Raeff, *Michael Speransky*, 330-40; M.A. Korf, *Zhizn' grafa Speranskom* (St. Petersburg, 1861), II, 159, 311.

84 Vinaver, "K voprosu," 52-68.

85 Raeff, *Michael Speransky*, 335.

86 Richard C. Wortman, *The Development of a Russian Legal Consciousness* (Chicago: University of Chicago Press, 1976), 43.

87 Ibid.; Mikhail M. Speranskii, *Obozrenie istoricheskikh svedenii o Svod Zakonov* (St. Petersburg, 1833), 55-56.

CHAPTER FOUR

FOREIGN INFLUENCES
ON RUSSIAN LEGAL CODIFICATION

One of the consistent debates in Russian history has been over the influence of foreigners in Russia. During the codification of Russian law under Speranskii two key areas show the influence of foreigners. Speranskii turned to European models for some of his reform efforts and the training of assistants because Russia was unable to provide domestic models for either. It was evident to Speranskii and Balug'ianskii by the end of 1827 that the compilation of the *PSZ* was too large and too complicated for the members of the Second Section to complete. They needed more members with better training in law. There had been attempts in the eighteenth and early nineteenth centuries at providing legal education, but these efforts were mainly directed at the sons of the nobility and produced few trained jurists. Most of the Russian jurists of the eighteenth and early nineteenth centuries received their training abroad. In the early nineteenth century, the lyceum at Tsarskoe Selo offered law as part of its curriculum, but few students pursued it or took it seriously. Since a lack of trained jurists was limiting the work of the Second Section, Balug'ianskii proposed sending young men to Europe for specialized training in law. Nicholas agreed to send a select group of young men for training at the University of Berlin under the direction of jurist Friedrich Savigny which was arranged through Balug'ianskii personal connections in Berlin.[1]

The best students from the theological seminaries in St. Petersburg and Moscow were selected and in 1828, six students went to Berlin to study. Even though Savigny supervised their work, he had very little direct involvement and left the actual instruction of the Russian students to his assistants and other faculty members. These students were to stay for two years then return to work in the Second Section and continue their studies at Russian universities. While in Berlin each student was provided with a stipend of 600 rubles annually. As correspondence between Speranskii and Balug'ianskii revealed in late 1828, this sum was four times lower than what was needed.[2] This seems to have been a chronic problem for Russian students studying abroad. In the middle of the eighteenth century, Semion E. Desnitskii and Ivan Tret'iakov often ran out of money while studying at the University of Glasgow under Adam Smith. Later, in the early nineteenth century, Second Section senior member Kunitsyn had to interrupt his education often at the University of Göttingen to find sources of income.[3]

In a memo from Speranskii to Balug'ianskii in 1829, it noted that the annual stipends increased dramatically from the original 600 rubles per year to 1800 rubles. By 1830 the stipend rose to 2700 rubles per student annually. Initially, the students were funded by the government, but by 1830 the Second Section itself was able to contribute.[4] Each year until 1835 Speranskii and Balug'ianskii sent between four and six students to Berlin for training. Upon the completion of their studies, the students were expected to take examinations over the subjects they had studied.

Speranskii and Balug'ianskii clearly outlined the course of study while in Berlin and after they returned to Russia. In the first year abroad the students were to be introduced to general principles concerning the juridical and political sciences. From there, Speranskii clearly laid out six specific areas to be studied in the first year. First, all students would study an overview of Russian legal history from the time of Vladimir to early nineteenth century. Second, all students had to study either Russian state law or Russian public law. Speranskii and Balug'ianskii tried to link Russian law to that of other nations, so the third area for study was Roman law and its theories on civil law. The fourth through sixth areas seemed less important but were recorded in Speranskii's proposal. The fourth area was a course on political economy, the fifth was a general history course, and the last was on foreign languages including Greek, Latin, German, French and English. The first year of study was very heavily focused on history which can be attributed to Savigny and his historical approach to law.[5]

The second year at the University of Berlin focused more on law. Speranskii drafted six areas for this year as well. The first area was on Russian civil law. Speranskii believed that a clear understanding of civil law was obviously one of the primary goals of the Second Section. The second area was on political laws and the third area was on the study of laws related to the finances of the empire. Once again areas four through six appeared to be less important. Area four was a course on Roman law. The fifth area was on Russian history and the last was on foreign languages.[6]

Once the students returned to Russia and the Second Section, their lessons continued. The third year continued to emphasize Russian civil law, Russian criminal law, national law, the history of Roman law, statistics, and foreign languages. Several of the senior members taught the students. For example, Kunitsyn taught Russian legal history and Klokov taught Russian state law. In addition, the students continued their study of foreign languages at their universities.[7]

The first group of students sent to Berlin were from St. Petersburg and Moscow theological seminaries. The three from St. Petersburg were Alexander Chekhovskii, Nikita Krylov and Aleksei Kunitsyn and the three from Moscow were Ivan Platonov, Iakov Platonov and Sergei Barshev. One of the first issues the students faced was that of money. They were initially poorly funded, as noted earlier, but eventually received adequate funds. Speranskii petitioned different government ministries for money for these students including the Ministry of Foreign Affairs and the Ministry of Public Enlightenment. This class and those to follow encountered other hardships during this time in Europe. At least two students between 1828 and 1835 died of consumption during their stay in Berlin. This was generally attributed to the poor conditions in which the students lived.[8]

Reports on the progress of the students flowed between Speranskii and Savigny. In late 1830, Savigny reported the fine progress of all students. He explained that for most of them it did not take very long to adjust to life in Berlin. He noted, though, that the major difficulty was the German language, but through language courses this was improving. While Russian seminaries attempted to teach foreign languages, these efforts, however, did not fully prepare the students for study abroad. Savigny especially noted one student in 1830. He applauded the talents and abilities of Peter Redkin who excelled in his studies in Berlin and later returned to Russia to become a prominent jurist.[9]

Later Redkin taught law at Moscow University in the 1840s to a generation of students who would be involved in the Great Reforms of the 1860s. W. Bruce Lincoln notes that Redkin and his students understood Hegelian philosophy so that "a heightened consciousness, gained through study and scientific inquiry, could enable them to take part in the great universal process of change, and that in turn affirmed their ability to improve the quality of life in Russia."[10]

Marc Raeff asserts, however, that as this process did not produce any profound thinkers, it did lead "to the establishment of jurisprudence and the history of law as academic disciplines in Russia."[11] For example, Balug'ianskii reported in 1836 a number of former students who were teaching law in Russia's universities. At St. Petersburg University Kalmykov, Kranikhfeld, and Iakov Barshev were teaching various areas of law. At Moscow University Redkin, Krylov, and Sergei Barshev were on the faculty. On the Faculty at Karkhov University were Aleksei Kunitsyn and Platonov while Ornatskii, Bogorodskii and Konstantin Nevolin occupied positions at Kiev University.[12]

Between 1828 and 1835, Speranskii and Balug'ianskii sent an average of six students per year to Berlin for training under Savigny and his historical school of law. From Savigny's notes, most students performed well and took up posts in the Second Section and later at Russian universities. This flow of students ended in 1835 when Balug'ianskii, Speranskii, and Peter Oldenburgskii received permission from Nicholas I to open the Imperial School of Jurisprudence in St. Petersburg.

This small group of students seemed to improved the study of law in Russia. Their improved legal skills helped greatly in the work of collection and deciphering. Even though their education focused primarily on Russian law, foreign legal ideas invariably influenced their thinking and their later teaching. The question that arose was to what extent did this foreign influence affect the compilation of the *PSZ* and the *SZ*? This was difficult to determine without analyzing all

30,920 laws and the backgrounds, educations, and philosophies of all members of the Second Section. However, archival records show that foreign legal principles influenced members of the Second Section in how they selected and arranged laws for the *PSZ*.

As Speranskii and the senior members of the Second Section carried out the work of compiling the *PSZ* and supervised the education abroad of some of the members, foreign legal models were considered from four European nations for several areas. These legal issues were left mainly to Speranskii and Korf. Even though the scope of the search of Russian archives was limited, Speranskii consulted foreign legal sources for comparisons and for justifications for his actions. In notes found in Speranskii's archival records, he referred to the legal systems of England, Austria, France, and Prussia as models for some of his projects.

His references to English law came in a subtle way. He copied an article from *The Courier* from March 10, 1826, concerning the criminal statutes of England.[13] This article was the transcript from a session of Parliament in the early 1820s. The Parliament member was proposing the consolidation or simplification of statutes concerning criminal law. However, little of this article discussed criminal laws specifically, rather it defended the practice of simplification, consolidation, collecting, and reorganizing bodies of English law. The member's rationale for this simplification was to make "the law which each individual in the country was bound to obey, should be understood, not by lawyers alone; but that it should be clear and intelligible to all."[14] This was the overarching principle that Speranskii and Nicholas I had expressed for the *PSZ*.

Some of his follow members of Parliament accused the author of fundamentally altering the law or changing it outright. The author defended his actions by referring to the words of Francis Bacon from over two centuries earlier. He claimed, as he believed Bacon had, that this proposal did "not lendeth to plowing up and planting again; for such a remove, I should not indeed for a perilous innovation."[15] Speranskii, further found common ground with English legal reform in Bacon's efforts of the sixteenth century. Elizabeth I ordered Bacon to draw "up a plan for reducing, ordering, and printing the statutes of the realm"[16] in 1577. This plan was revised in 1593, 1597, 1610, 1653, 1666 and so on. It was clear from this article that Speranskii found a common bond with the development of English law. It was particularly important for Speranskii to find examples where the law was simply reordered, collected, and published. Speranskii's drive for a clear and accessible law code for Russia seemed to find justification in two hundred years of English legal history.

Bacon additionally referred to the influence of foreign laws in England. While he acknowledged that foreign laws occasionally would be more appropriate for England, he maintained that these laws would not be accepted by English lawyers or common people. Bacon offended many in the House of Commons for his views on the law, and while he was not tried he agreed to pay a fine in 1621 and was "barred from holding office, and forbidden to come near any place where a court was sitting, lest he contaminate it."[17] He concluded that even though some English laws may be flawed, they were still English laws.[18] Similarly, Speranskii knew of the problems with the *PSZ*, but it was Russian law.

While the majority of the foreign legal influence fell upon the active code of laws, the *SZ*, English legal history provided Speranskii with the basis for collecting and reorganizing the laws into a massive collection. Even though Bacon maintained that it was not his position to alter English law, it was apparent that Speranskii and the Second Section did change some laws as they were added to the *PSZ*. Other areas of Russian law were influenced by other European nations.

Over the 176 year period covered in the *PSZ*, inheritance laws in Russia changed frequently. Korf and his assistants were responsible for this section on personal law. Korf struggled with the ordering and the inclusion of these laws. Many of the laws were unclear concerning the different lines of inheritance. Korf looked to foreign models for ideas on how to rationalize a mass of confusing legislation. Part of the confusion stemmed from Peter I's change of the law of primogeniture. As a result of the conflict with his son Aleksei and the heir's death, Peter changed the law to stipulate that the emperor or empress should select his or her heir prior to death.[19] This had a dramatic political impact as well as a ripple effect concerning inheritance law. Later in the eighteenth century, though, the law of royal succession and inheritance was returned to the more traditional pattern.

As Korf and his assistants tried to make sense of this mass of contradictory legislation, he looked at Austrian, French, and Prussian models for direction. From Austrian law, Speranskii and Korf copied several sections from the thirteenth chapter of the Austrian Civil Code concerning inheritance law. From the records of the weekly meetings of the Second Section during the summer of 1826, Korf recorded his efforts to order Russian inheritance laws properly.[20] The section of the Austrian code that was cited contained fifteen laws that were numbered 735 to 750.[21]

From these statutes, the second through sixth lines of inheritance were clearly outlined. While the first line referred to direct inheritance, the others explored different situations concerning no male heirs, nephews, cousins, and other distant relatives.[22]

Korf seemed to find more answers in the French and Prussian legal examples. He cited at length the *Code Napoleon* of 1804 (revision of 1800 version) as an example of proper inheritance law. The text was from Book 3, Chapter 1, Sections 4 and 5. He quoted sections that address directly the passing of property from one party to another in the case of death. In addition, the text had both French and Russian versions side by side. The fourth section outlined abstractly the idea of inheritance law. It was remarkably similar to the Austrian version. It offered schemes for inheritance when the lines were muddled.[23]

The fifth section was entitled "On the inheritance of relations in a lateral line." This document clearly outlined attempts to locate appropriate heirs to property. For example, appropriate heirs were searched for on the man's side of the family first. If no suitable heirs were found, then a search of the woman's side would be done. Korf did not find suitable models in the French code, perhaps, because as one historian calls it the "prototype of what has come to be called social engineering."[24] Since the French code did not fit with Russia's legal heritage, the Second Section looked elsewhere for models. Korf and Speranskii had worked on this subject quite extensively in 1826 and 1827.[25] By late 1827, they looked to Prussian examples to see if they could find proper models.

Korf cited the Prussian law codes on the same subject.[26] Korf provided a German and Russian version of this section of the code. This code did not provide Speranskii and Korf with anything more than the French or Austrian codes had concerning inheritance law. It simply went through logical scenarios for lines of inheritance. However, all of these foreign models provided Korf and Speranskii with a justification for an abstract code of laws. The purpose of the *PSZ* was to collect the laws of the empire and provide a basis for an active code of laws. It was evident that the laws on inheritance in particular were so muddled that Speranskii and Korf were forced to look at foreign models to formulate some general principles.

In the end, the compilation of the *PSZ* was unextraordinary accomplishment for Speranskii and the Russian Empire. The understanding of the purpose of this collection varied widely. For Nicholas I it was a sampling of historical laws in preparation for the *SZ*. For Speranskii and Balug'ianskii initially wanted a complete collection, but quickly limited the scope of the project. The work itself fell into two categories. First, it was evident that the Second Section relied heavily on the work of previous commissions. Second, much of the work of reviewing old lists and adding new laws by searching archives and other depositories was left to the assistants. Lastly, the influence of English law on the structure and justification of the *PSZ* came clearly through Speranskii's hand. Austrian, French and Prussian legal models influenced many areas of law including those on inheritance.

As the Second Section moved to its work on the *SZ* so did their use of foreign legal models. The Second Section will undertake the task of finding those laws that were still in force and arranging them topically into eight books which filled fifteen volumes. This was a complex task and the training of assistants continued as well as the reliance on foreign legal models.[27] As mentioned in the previous section, groups of students were being sent abroad to study law and then return to work in the Second Section. Most of their education abroad took place in the first years of the Second Section while their domestic legal education continued during the compilation of the *SZ*. Most of the students who returned from Europe had received two years of legal training. As they began their work in the Second Section, they continued their studies at St. Petersburg University under direction of senior member of the Second Section.

The course of instruction for students in Russian universities was a blend of what they had done in European universities and specific courses on Russian law. Since these students were now working for the Second Section, their coursework was limited to three areas. First, as in Europe, they studied Roman law. It is evident that Speranskii and Balug'ianskii placed a special importance upon Roman law. Speranskii believed that the Russian legal traditional came indirectly from Roman law.[28] The second course of instruction was in Latin and Greek. Latin proved useful for reading the Roman texts and Greek was important for examining the Byzantine origins of the Russian legal system. The third course was the more practical of the lessons. It focused on Russian law based on the material collected by the Second Section. This instruction was integrally related to the work the students undertook as assistants in the Second Section.[29] Archival sources show that the curriculum for advanced students included a variety of other subjects. The senior members of the Second Section who taught a majority of the courses were Plisov and Kunitsyn. They taught the most advanced students a wide range of subjects including "Russian jurisprudence, political economy, history and statistics."[30] As an example, senior member Konstantin Arsenev taught a course on the history of "the first period from the invasion of the Northern people in the Western Roman Empire during the reign of Karl the Great."[31] Similarly, Plisov taught a course on the theory and science of state finance.[32]

One of the key problems with the development of law as a profession in Russia, however, was the role of young noblemen. Higher education was not popular among noble families, but early in Alexander's reign Speranskii initiated reforms of the civil service that linked advancement in government service to education, as noted in Chapter Two. By the time these students in the Second Section, who were predominantly of common origin (sons of clergy especially) took positions in the universities more noblemen were enrolled, but serious study of law remained rare.[33] After the students had completed their work in the Second Section, the intention was for them to continue their studies and receive a doctorate in law and eventually take faculty positions in Russian universities to teach law. Speranskii and Balug'ianskii wanted to establish a group of trained jurists to create a domestic legal profession. This began as these students completed their work in the Second Section. Many of the students took positions at St. Petersburg University and Moscow University while many Russian universities still lacked law professors and students.[34]

Speranskii and Balug'ianskii took this idea a step further in 1835 when they helped establish the Imperial School of Jurisprudence in St. Petersburg. This same year Nicholas I issued the University Statute which made the teaching of law a primary concern for Russian universities.[35] Sons of noblemen were more attracted to the environment of the elite Imperial School of Jurisprudence rather than the universities. The serious study of law here was only beginning but because of the personal preferences of the director Prince Peter Oldenburgskii, many students developed keen interests in music and art.[36]

The attempts at legal education by Speranskii and the Second Section were among the first that truly succeeded. There had been numerous attempts at legal education in the eighteenth and early nineteenth centuries, but few had any practical results. However, poorly-educated civil servants, usually of noble birth, still plagued the Russian administration. Once Speranskii and Alexander I reformed the civil service and linked education to advancement in government service in the early nineteenth century, the nobility especially began to pursue education.[37]

Alexander I founded the lyceum at Tsarskoe Selo in 1809 as institution for the nobility. From this pool of graduates he was trying to fill his bureaucracy, but specific legal training was not emphasized. The only institution that taught law specifically was Moscow University. When Nicholas took the throne in 1825, he and Speranskii agreed that Russia needed "knowledgeable judges and jurists."[38] In 1825, there was no systematic domestic legal training in Russia. All of the professors of law in Russia were either foreign experts hired to teach in Russian universities or were Russians who had been sent abroad for legal training. So, the first generation of law professors and trained jurists came through the Second Section. When these students had completed their work in the Second Section and their later studies, they took positions to teach law in Russian universities. They were to teach law to the emerging legal profession in Russia. Many of their students in the 1840s and 1850s would be involved in the Judicial Reforms of 1864.

Nicholas laid out clearly that these students were to learn laws and not abstract legal principles. He was more concerned that they memorized laws and sections of the *SZ*, rather than obtain an abstract understanding of the law. It was clear, though, that Russian university legal education was erratic and often incomplete. Real systematic legal education did not begin in Russia until the founding of the Imperial School of Jurisprudence in St. Petersburg in 1835.[40]

The Imperial School of Jurisprudence was designed to train young noblemen in the law at the secondary level in preparation for bureaucratic careers. There are two striking differences between this school and the legal education abroad Speranskii and Balug'ianskii had sponsored through the Second Section. First, this school was only open to noblemen while those sent abroad were the academic elite from the seminaries and were often the sons of priests (like Speranskii). Also, the Imperial School of Jurisprudence was designed for boys from the age of twelve to eighteen while those sent abroad were usually around twenty years old.[41]

As a result of the educational developments in the early nineteenth century and especially those carried out by the Second Section, many trained jurists began to take posts in the Russian government and academia by the 1840s and 1850s. This emerging legal profession, that would be so important in the legal reforms of the 1860s, had its origins in the educational initiatives of the Second Section.[42]

It was evident that the students involved in the Second Section spent much of their time reviewing and studying legal concepts from many nations. This association with foreign legal sources had an impact on the *SZ* as it had on the earlier *PSZ*. As noted earlier, in the discussion of the tenth volume on civil law, French models were used heavily.

However, other nations' legal systems also proved to be influential on this most controversial book.

Much like the *PSZ*, the Second Section relied on foreign legal models to help organize and rationalize Russian law for the current digest. P.M. Maikov noted that the Second Section relied on current foreign legal models as well as older ones as they compiled the *SZ*. Swedish laws from nearly a century before provided a key basis for civil law in Russia. A Swedish manifesto from 1736 was consolidated and included in the civil law section of the *SZ* and then afterwards Russian laws that were similar were included as what Maikov calls "helping laws."[43]

Austrian law also played a key role in the shaping of civil laws. Austrian legal principles from as far back as 1786 influenced how Speranskii established norms for hereditary law. As noted earlier, Russian hereditary law was confused and Speranskii tried to rationalize it along the lines laid out by Austrian law codes. Speranskii was especially concerned with the transfer of land from one generation to another and the increasingly constant division of large estates into smaller and smaller sections. He attempted to establish a single heir as the norm for Russian hereditary law.[44]

Prussian law was also especially important because legal codes from the late eighteenth century influenced the *SZ* in a variety of areas. For instance, Prussian legal principles concerning the legal relationship between parents and children were especially important. A second important area of influence was in the defining of the legal status of monasteries, churches and religious orders.[45] While the Russian Orthodox Church was officially under state control since the era of Peter the Great, the legal status of provincial religious institutions was often in question. In general, the Prussian law code of the late eighteenth century was quite influential. Speranskii used it extensively to establish new legal norms in Russia for "the foundation of various offices, concerning taxation and duty, concerning forestry, the mining business and others."[46]

French legal ideas came mainly from the French *Code Napoleon* of 1800. For the *SZ* four key areas were especially important. First, as discussed earlier, was the interest in civil law and civil proceedings which had a direct impact on the tenth volume of the *SZ*. The second major area was concerning criminal law which was contained in the fifteenth volume of the Russian digest. The third area dealt with commercial legal proceedings which were contained in the seventh volume. The last area upon which French legal ideas had a tremendous influence was on forestry law which was also contained in the seventh volume of the *SZ*.[47]

Speranskii drew heavily from the French code for sources on criminal law. He was particularly concerned with crimes against the state. The first area concerned crimes against the monarchy. As a result of the Decembrist Uprising in 1825, Nicholas was afraid of another revolt against the monarchy, as noted earlier. The French were also fearful of revolts against the monarchy because of their recent revolution in 1789. Speranskii adopted into the criminal law section of the *SZ* a provision that any crimes against the monarchy would require death as the penalty.[48]

The second important area revolved around the roles of accomplices and participants in crime. Speranskii adopted the notion that the participant and accomplice in a crime against the state were to be tried and punished equally. The normal term of imprisonment was ten to twenty years. Along the same lines, Speranskii believed that those people who knew of a crime, but failed to take action to stop it faced a penalty of six to ten years in prison. For those who knew of a crime after the fact, but failed to report it, trial and prison sentences could follow. In this case, exceptions were made for reporting on family members. Speranskii agreed with the French code on the point that people should not be forced to inform on their own families even in the case of a crime against the state.[49]

The final two areas that Speranskii adopted from the French code were leaving the scene of a crime, or abandonment of a crime against the state, and espionage against the state. Speranskii believed that the failure to remain at a crime scene contributed to the seriousness of the crime. As for espionage, Speranskii concurred with the French code that perpetrators of these crimes should face the toughest of penalties possible.[50] Other European law codes influenced the *SZ* as well.

While English law served as a justification for Speranskii's compiling the *PSZ*, it also had a direct impact on how the *SZ* was arranged. English law had two key influences:

> *1) laws (rules) or regulations, an account in brief on pronunciation, and*
> *2) examples of codes of laws decrees (cases), and explanation of these rules.*[51]

Speranskii's reliance upon foreign legal models produced a number of results. He was able to fill in many of the gaps in Russian law. Foreign legal ideas also reshaped how Speranskii viewed the class system in Russia. Speranskii laid out clearly the four estates of Russia: nobility, clergy, townspeople, and rural folk. The first three classes were well-defined and had a long history in Russia. However, rural folk had never been classified this way. Speranskii failed to recognize the distinction between free peasants, serfs, church peasants and state peasants. The social and political structure of the peasantry was complex, and Speranskii's omission, according to Raeff, was an attempt to equalize the complex rights granted to the numerous varieties of peasantry.[52] Speranskii's reordering of the social system in Russia violated the historical approach to legal reform he had adopted from the Prussian jurist Friedrich Savigny while Speranskii was in exile in Siberia. He seemed to ignore the historical trends in Russia. Speranskii eliminated the finer distinctions between the rural folk which left many in the Second Section confused about how to arrange the *SZ*, especially those laws which applied to certain classes of peasants.[53]

While earlier in Speranskii's career, he and Alexander I had discussed the eventual freeing of the serfs, by Nicholas I's era this was no longer a topic for discussion. Speranskii, as in all of his reform efforts throughout his career, wanted order, regularity, efficiency and simplicity. It was clear that he was simplifying the relationships between classes to have a clear and efficient law code. This desire for efficiency was reflected in how the *SZ* was arranged. Many laws were summaries of one or more laws. Only extracts or small paragraphs were used to define the subject of each law. Speranskii thought judges and jurists would then refer to the *PSZ* for the full text of the law. The references Speranskii used in the *SZ* were frequently too vague. Often one law was not clearly cited so to find it in the *PSZ* resulted in either finding numerous laws cited or not being able to find the correct law at all.[54]

M.M. Vinaver and L. Kasso both agree that Speranskii accidentally and intentionally introduced new legal norms into the *SZ*. On the one hand, Speranskii unknowingly introduced new legal norms by condensing, summarizing and simplifying laws. Yet, it was clear that Speranskii introduced elements of his "Plan of 1809" into the *SZ*. He knew very well that his plan was never enacted as law despite the fact the Council of State had adopted it.[55] An explanation for Speranskii's introduction of new legal norms whether direct or not was clearly explained by historian and jurist N.M. Korkunov. He asserts that while the *SZ* was theoretically a reference work for judges and jurists to use to find summaries and citations of the full texts in the *PSZ*, Speranskii believed that the *SZ* should be able to stand on its own as the legal foundation for the Russian empire.[56] The result was that Nicholas began to reject the *PSZ* as the source or basis of the *SZ*. He also wanted the *SZ* to stand alone and felt that the *PSZ* was merely an historical exercise. Nicholas' rationale was a desire for a simple concise code of law to maintain his control of Russia. Raeff asserts that eventually after amendments were made in the *SZ* "it became, in fact, the official interpretation of Russian law."[57] The key word here is interpretation. The *SZ* was no longer the reference work or digest of the most current laws in Russia, but rather it had developed, whether intentionally or not, into a kind of code of law for Russia.

As mentioned earlier, though, one issue that continued to plague the Second Section as they put together the *PSZ* and the *SZ*, was provincial or local laws. Speranskii collected local and native laws recognizing the complexity of legal traditions in the Russian Empire. Theoretically, all subjects of the Russian Empire should be ruled by Russian law, but there were exceptions. Raeff claims though that many primitive peoples, like the nomads of Siberia, had a difficult time adhering to imperial law. With the speedy codification of law in Russia, so was its implementation on all of the peoples of Russia.

In conclusion, the *SZ* was both good and bad for Russia. It provided jurists and judges with a reference work with which to do their work. They were able to find relevant laws for their cases more easily, and it also served as one of the textual basis, with the *PSZ*, for the emerging legal profession in Russia. Without this foundation, the legal reforms of the 1860s would have been difficult, if not impossible. However, the errors and alterations of the *SZ* changed Russian law significantly. It also only served as the digest of Russian law until the era of the Great Reforms of the 1860s partially because the Second Section failed to keep up with the annual updates. It was also not sophisticated enough to accommodate the rapid changes taking place in Russian society, government and economy by the middle of the nineteenth century. Raeff concludes that Speranskii believed that a clear set of laws could help shape the moral and economic behavior of nations; that Speranskii believed such laws could help shape Russia's future so long as they did not contradict the nation's earlier legal history. In carrying out his last major legal project, Speranskii continued to believe as he had as a young man, namely, that through better law he could help perfect the Russian state and people.[58]

Notes

[1] Raeff, *Michael Speransky*, 329-30; P.M. Maikov, " Speranskii i studenty zakonovedeniia", Russkii Ve*stnik* 8 (1899) : 609-10.

[2] Maikov, "Speranskii i studenty", 610-12; Mikhail M., "Vsepodanneishii doklad o studentov pravovedeniia v Berlinskii universitet," September 4, 1829, RNB, F. 731: M.M., op. 1, d. 1144, 11. 1-2.

[3] A.H. Brown, "The Father of Russian Jurisprudence: The Legal Thought of S.E. Desnitskii," in *Russian Law: Historical and Political Perspectives*, ed. W.E. Butler (Leyden: A.N. Sijhoff, 1977), 93-115; Barry Hollingsworth, "A.P. Kunitsyn and the Social Movement in Russia under Alexander I," *Slavonic and East European Review* 43 (1964) : 114-29.

4 Mikhail M., "Vsepodanneishii doklad o studentov," September 4, 1829, RNL, F. 731: M.M., op. 1, d. 1144, 11. 2-3.

5 Maikov, "Speranskii i studenty", 615.

6 Ibid.; "O studentakh kandidatakh pravovedeniia," 1828, RGIA, F. 1261: Vtoroe otdelenie sobstvennoi E.i.v. kantseliarii, op. 1, d. 7a, 11, 1-15.

7 Maikov, "Speranskii i studenty," 616.

8 Ibid., 246; "Otpusk summ na putevyia izderzhki i na soderzhanie ikh Berline, perepiska v Berlinsimi Professorami predmetakh takzhe o vozrashchenii v Rossiu pervykh 7go studentov," 1828, RGIA, F. 1261: Vtoroe otdelenie sobstvennoi E.i.v. kantseliarii, op. 1, d. 7b, 11. 1-10.

9 Mikhail M. Speranskii, "Vsepodanneishii doklad o studentakh pravovedeniia obuchaushchikhsia v Berline," November 6, 1830, RNB, F. 731: M.M. Speranskii, op. 1, d. 1145, 11. 1-3; Maikov, "Speranskii i studenty," 624-25.

10 W. Bruce Lincoln, In the Vang*uard of Reform: Russia's Enlightened Bureaucrats, 1825-1861* (DeKalb, IL: Northern Illinois University Press, 1982), 70.

11 Raeff, *Michael Speransky*, 327-28; Maikov, "Speranskii i studenty", 680-82.

12 Maikov, "Speranskii i studenty", 680-82.

13 "Vypiski iz prusskikh, angliskikh, i fratsuzskikh ugolovnikh zakonov", 1831, RGIA, F. 1251: Bumagi M.M. Speranskago, op. 1, d. 143, 11. 22-28.

14 Ibid., 22.

15 Ibid., 24.

16 Ibid., 26.

17 Colin Rhys Lovell, *English Constitutional and Legal History: A Survey* (New York: Oxford University Press, 1962), 299.

18 "Vypiski iz prusskikh, angliskikh, i fratsuzskikh ugolovnikh zakonov," 1831 RGIA, F. 1251: Bumagi M.M. Speranskago, op. 1, d. 143, 1. 23.

19 V.O. Kluichevskii, *Peter the Great* (New York: Vintage Books, 1961), 106-111.

20 "Memorii o trudakh chinovnikom IIgo otdeleniia sobstvennoi ego imperatorskago velichestva kantseliarii zanimaushchikhsia svobami," May 12, 1826, RGIA, F. 1251: Bumagi M.M. Speranskago, op. 1, d. 86, 1. 70.

21 "Vypiski iz inostranikh zakonov o nasledstve v voskhodiashchie linii," 1826, RGIA, F. 1251: Bumagi M.M. Speranskago, op. 1, d. 61, 11, 2-5.

22 Ibid., 2-9.

23 Ibid., 17-19.

24 Donald R. Kelly, *Historians and the Laws in Postrevolutionary France* (Princeton: Princeton University Press, 1984), 43.

25 "Vypiski iz inostranikh zakonov o nasledstve v voskhodiashchie linii," 1826 RGIA, F. 1251: Bumagi M.M. Speranskago, op. 1, d. 61, 11. 18-20.

26 "Vypiski iz inostranikh zakonov o nasledstve v voskhodiashchei linii", May 12, 1826, RGIA, F. 1251: Bumagi M.M. Speranskago, op. 1, d. 61, 11, 10-17; "Memorii o trudakh chinovnikom IIgo otdeleniia sobstvennoi ego imperatorskago velichestva kantseliarii zanimaushchikhsia svobami," May 15, 1826, RGIA, F. 1251: Bumagi M.M. Speranskago, op. 1, d. 86, 1. 70.

28 P.M. Maikov, "Speranskii i studenty zakonovedeniia," *Russkii Vestnik* 8 (1899) : 621; M.M. Speranskii, "O zakonakh rimskikh i razlichii ikh ot zakonov rossiskikh," *Russkaia Starina* 15 (1876) : 592-97.

29 Maikov, "Speranskii i studenty", 621.

30 "Zaniatiia studentov v universitete," October 18, 1828, RGIA, F. 1251: Bumagi M.M. Speranskago, op. 1, d. 86b, 1. 78; Maikov, "Speranskii i studenty", 677.

31 "Zaniatiia studentov v universitete," October 18, 1828, RGIA, F. 1251: Bumagi M.M. Speranskago, op. 1, d. 86b, 1. 78b.

32 Ibid.

33 Wortman, *Legal Consciousness*, 48.

34 Maikov, "Speranskii i studenty", 677.

35 James T. Flynn, *The University Reform of Alexander I, 1802-1835* (Washington, D.C.: Catholic University Press, 1988), 216-40.

36 Allen Sinel, "The Socialization of the Russian Bureacratic Elite, 1811-1917: Life at Tsarskoe Selo Lyceum and the Imperial School of Jurisprudence," *Russian History* 3 : 1 (1976) : 1-31.

37 Wortman, *Legal Consciousness,* 41.

38 Ia. Barshev, *Istoricheskaia zapiska o sodeistvii Vtorogo Otdeleniia sobstvennoi ego I.V. Kantseliarii razvitii iuridicheskikh nauk v Rossii* (St. Petersburg, 1876), 8; Sinel, "Socialization," 1-6.

39 Wortman, *Legal Consciousness*, 45-49.

40 Ibid., 45-49.

41 Ibid., 48-50.

42 Brian Levin-Stankevich, "The Transfer of Legal Technology and Culture: Law Professionals in Tsarist Russia," in *Russia's Missing Middle Class: The Professions in Russian History* ed. Harley D. Balzer (Armonk, NY: M.E. Sharpe, 1996), 223-228.

43 P.M. Maikov, *O Svode Zakonov Rossiiskoi Imperii* (St. Petersburg, 1905), 67-68.

44 "Vypiska iz Avstriiskago Grazhdanskago Ulozheniia", 1831, RGIA, F. 1251: Bumagi M.M. Speranskago, op. 1, d. 61, 11, 2-9; Maikov, *O Svode,* 68-70.

45 Maikov, *O Svode,* 75.

46 Ibid., 70.

47 Ibid., 70-71.

48 "Des crimes contre l'Etat," 1832, RGIA, F. 1251: Bumagi M.M. Speranskago, op. 1, d. 143, 11. 34-35.

49 Ibid., 36-37.

50 Ibid., 37-38.

51 Maikov, *O Svode,* 71.

52 Raeff, *Michael Speransky,* 336.

53 Ibid., 336-37; Speranskii, *Obozrenie,* 30-45.

54 Raeff, *Michael Speransky,* 338.

55 Ibid.; L.A. Kasso, "K istorii svoda zakonov grazhdanskikh," *Zhurnal Ministerstva Iustitsii* (March 1904): 53-70; M.M. Vinaver, "K voprosu ob istochnikakh X toma Svoda Zakonov," *Zhurnal Ministerstva Iustitsii* (June 1897): 87-102.

56 N.M. Korkunov, "Znachenie Svoda Zakonov," *Sbornik statei N.M. Korkunova 1877-1897* (St. Petersburg, 1898), 77.

57 Raeff, *Michael Speransky,* 339.

58 Ibid., 343-44.

CONCLUSION

Marc Raeff concludes that "the codification is a culmination and the highest expression of Speransky's basic political tenets".[1] Indeed, throughout Speranskii's career he had desired a clear and concise set of laws for Russia. His last major bureaucratic project created two extraordinary collections of Russian law. The *PSZ* was the collection of past laws issued by the monarch since the *Ulozhenie* of 1649 to until mid-December 1825. The *SZ* was a digest of the laws in effect in 1833. Moreover, several general conclusions can be drawn concerning Speranskii and his role in the development of law in Russia in the second quarter of the nineteenth century.

Eighteenth century codification efforts failed to produce a new code or even a complete collection of laws for Russia. The ten commissions called to codify Russian law before 1826 did not always have their goals properly defined, lacked properly-trained officials, and received only occasional support from the monarch. The most productive commissions served under Peter I and Catherine II. Nearly every commission produced small and incomplete collections which were never implemented. Speranskii, however, would use all of these previous collections as he compiled the *PSZ* and the *SZ* in the 1820s and 1830s.

Speranskii was the driving force behind the codification work. His background and career before 1826 helped shape his approach to this massive project at the end of this career. He was the son of a priest and excelled in his academic pursuits which helped him enter and rise in the bureaucratic ranks. From 1802 to 1812 he experienced his greatest period of influence on Alexander I as he drafted reform plans for the "liberal" emperor. In 1809, Speranskii drafted his most controversial reform plan, commonly known as the "Plan of 1809."[2] This plan, Speranskii's pro-French leanings, and the rising crisis with Napoleon led to his exile in 1812. While in exile in Siberia, Speranskii studied many different academic areas as he petitioned the emperor to return to St. Petersburg. His successful governorship in Penza and his reform of the Siberian administration proved his loyalty and value as a bureaucrat to Alexander I. By the early 1820s, Speranskii had returned to St. Petersburg to continue the work of codification. His association with several Decembrists in 1825 placed him in a precarious political position. He again proved his loyalty to the new emperor, Nicholas I, and began work in the Second Section under Mikhail A. Balug'ianskii in 1826.

Throughout Speranskii's career his political and legal thought went through several phases. His early writing was more philosophical and discussed "liberal" ideas like liberty, constitutionalism, and freedom. His "Plan of 1809" borrowed heavily from the French *Code Napoleon* of 1800 and focused on three key issues. He discussed different forms of government for Russia, individual rights, and the possibility of representative assemblies in Russia. This plan helped lead to his exile. While away from the capital and after his return, his writing was less philosophical and more practical. He had adopted the historical approach to law based on his reading the works of Prussian jurist Friedrich Savigny. Late in his career he wrote about the purpose of an orderly legal system. He believed that "the aims of legislation are: the preservation of being, the direction of all forces toward the truth, the direction of the will toward the good, and the improvement of existence."[3] Speranskii's drive for a rational legal system and the "perfection" of Russian society inspired his work on the *PSZ* and the *SZ.*

The Commission on Laws produced journals on law and a survey of laws during Alexander's reign. The Commission's most productive period was from 1815 to 1822, and Speranskii and the Second Section used these collections in their compilation of the *PSZ* and *SZ.* Once the Second Section was called in 1826 Speranskii directed much of the work but held no official position. The hierarchy of the Second Section had Balug'iandkii as the official head, several senior members;

usually between four and six members depending on the project. The senior members relied heavily upon the assistants who were often anonymous in the weekly reports, and usually numbered between fifteen and twenty depending upon the project. The four key members were Balug'ianskii, Alexander P. Kunitsyn, Modest A. Korf, and Konstantin I. Arsenev. Their backgrounds, educations, and careers leading to service in the Second Section in 1826 were quite varied. Their diversity brought a variety of specialties to the Second Section that would be crucial for the production of the *PSZ* and the *SZ*.

The publication of the *PSZ* in 1830 and the *SZ* in 1833 the were results of a lifetime of work on legal issues for Speranskii. The *PSZ* is an impressive collection of laws of the Russian Empire from the *Ulozhenie* of 1649 to December 12, 1825 inclusive. Its purpose was to be an historical legal foundation from which a current digest of laws could be drawn. The *PSZ* also served as one of the textual basis for the emerging legal profession in 1840s and 1850s. More recently, the *PSZ* has been a valuable primary source for historians and other scholars who study Russian history from the late seventeenth through the early nineteenth centuries. The work needed to compile this massive collection required great organizational skills on the part of Speranskii and the senior members of the Second Section. In addition, the assistants were required to carry out much of the work. Many of the assistants were sent abroad to obtain the specialized legal training necessary to complete the compilation of the *PSZ*. Foreign legal models influenced both the *PSZ* and the *SZ*. For the former, Speranskii found models for several of its sections in Prussian, Austrian, and French models. He also found justification for the scope and the organization of the *PSZ* in English law from the sixteenth and seventeenth centuries.

The *SZ* served as the digest of active laws for the Russian Empire beginning in 1835. This collection was divided topically rather than chronologically like the *PSZ*. The selection of the laws for inclusion demanded a more specialized knowledge of law. By the time the *SZ* was being compiled many of the assistants who has been sent abroad for legal training were now working the Second Section and continuing their studies at Russian universities. This system of sending students abroad was abandoned in 1835 as Speranskii and Balug'ianskii helped in the founding of the Imperial School of Jurisprudence in St. Petersburg in the same year. Since there were gaps in certain areas of Russian law, like civil law, Speranskii incorporated foreign legal principles and some of his own earlier ideas to help construct new legal norms for Russia.

In conclusion, the compilation of the *PSZ* and the *SZ* in the 1830s was, as Raeff concludes earlier, the fullest expression of Speranskii's political ideas. These two collections were monumental achievements for Speranskii and the Russian Empire. The *PSZ* provided the historical basis for the study of Russian law in the nineteenth century. During Speranskii's later career he served Nicholas I loyally as he completed the compilation of the law. His early career and legal philosophy occasionally attracted disfavor from the emperor, but his last great bureaucratic effort showed that he had learned to be a loyal servant of the state.

Today, as noted earlier, it still stands as a valuable primary source for historians studying Russia's past. The *SZ* stood as the active digest of laws of the Russian Empire until the era of the Great Reforms in the 1860s. These two collections were Speranskii's last and greatest contribution to the Russian government, without which the reforms of the 1860s would have difficult, if not impossible.

NOTES

[1] Marc Raeff, *Michael Speransky: Statesman of Imperial Russia, 1772-1839* (The Hague: Martinus Nijhoff, 1957), 344.

[2] Mikhail M. Speranskii, "Vvedenie k ulozheniu gosudarstvennikh zakonov (1809g.)," in *Plan gosudarstvennago preobrazovanniia grafa M.M. Speranskago* (Moscow, 1905), 1-120 and M.M. Speranskii, *Proekty i zapiski* ed. S.N. Valk (Moscow-Leningrad, 1961), 143-221.

[3] Mikhail M. Speranskii, "O korennikh zakonakh gosudarstva," in *Proekty i zapiski* ed. S.N. Valk (Moscow-Leningrad, 1961), 37.

BIBLIOGRAPHY

Archival and Manuscript:
Arkhiv Akademii Nauk, St. Petersburg
Fond 117: K.I. Arsenev

Rossiiskaia Natsionalnaia Biblioteka, otdel rukopisei, St. Petersburg
Fond 637: K.G. Repinskii
Fond 731: M.M. Speranskii

Rossiiskii Gosudarstvennii Istoricheskii Arkhiv, St. Petersburg
Fond 1251: Bumagi M.M. Speranskago
Fond 1260: Kommissiia sostavlenie zakonov
Fond 1261: Vtoroe otdelenie sobstvennoi E.i.v. kantseliarii
Fond 1405: Ministerstva iustitsii

Published:
Arsenev, K.K. "Iz vospominanii." *Golos Minuvshchego*
2 (1915): 117-29.
　　　　"Vospominaniia K.K. Arsenev ob Uchilishche Pravovodeniia
1849-1855 gg." *Russkaia Starina* 50 : 4 (1886): 199-220.

Balugianskii, M.A. "Rassuzhdenie ob uchrezhdenii gubernii." *Sbornik
Imperatorskogo Russkago Istoricheskogo Obshchestva* 90 (nd):
214-74.

Blagoveshchenskii, A. "Istoriia metod nauki zakonovedeniia v XVIII i XIX v." *Zhurnal Ministerstva Narodogo Prosveshcheniia* 6 (1835): 375-441; 7 (1835): 42-52.

Catherine II, Empress. *The Grand Instructions to the Commissioners Appointed to Frame a New Code of Laws for the Russian Empire: Composed by Her Imperial Majesty Catherine II Empress of All the Russias.* Translated by Michael Tatishcheff. London: T. Jeffreys, 1768.

Catherine II's Charters of 1785 to the Nobility and the Towns. Translated and edited by David Griffiths and George E. Munro. Bakersfield, CA: Charles Schlacks, Jr. Publisher, 1991.

Desnitskii, S.E. "Proposal for the Establishment of Legislative, Judicial, and Executive Power in the Russian Empire." In *Russia Under Catherine the Great: Volume I: Selected Documents on Government and Society.* Edited by Paul Dukes, 47-68. Newtonville, MA: Oriental Research Partners, 1978.

Griffiths, David & Karen Griffiths, trans. and eds., with intro. Eduard Winter. "M.M. Speranskii As Viewed in L.H. Jacob's Unpublished Autobiography". *Canadian-American Slavic Studies* 9 : 4 (Winter 1975): 481-541.

Gorchakov, A.M. "Litseiskie tektskii: Entisklopediia prav." *Krasnyi Arkhiv* 80 : 1 (1937): 75-206.

Hellie, Richard. ed. and trans., *The Muscovite Law Code (Ulozhenie) of 1649.* 2 vols. Irvine, CA: Charles Schlacks, Jr., Publisher, 1988-89.

Kunitsyn, Aleksandr P. "O Konstitutsii." *Syn Otechestva* 45 (1818); 202-210.
     "O Rossiiskogo Pravo." *Syn Otechestva* 51 (1819): 242-52.
     Pravo Estestvennoe. 2 vols. St. Petersburg, 1818, 1820. Also in Shchipanov, I. Ia. ed. *Russkie prosvetiteli (Ot Radishcheva do Dekabristov): Sobranie proizendenii v dvukh tomakh.* Moscow, 1966.

Meshcherskii, V.P. *Moi Vospominaniia.* 2 vols. St. Petersburg, 1897-98.

Molchanov, M.M. "Aleksandr Nikolaevich Serov v vospomnaniiakh starago pravoveda." *Russkaia Starina* 8 (August 1883): 331-60.

Montesquieu, Baron de. *The Spirit of Laws.* 2 vols. Translated by Thomas Nugent. New York: Colonial Press, 1900.

Pobedonostsev, K.P. *Dlia nemnogikh: otryvki iz shkol'nago dnevnika 1842-1845 g.* St. Petersburg, 1885.

Polnoe Sobranie Zakonov Rossiiskoi Imperii. 1st ser. 45 vols. St. Petersburg, 1830; 2nd ser. 55 vols. St. Petersburg, 1830-84.

Savigny, Friedrich Karl. *Of the Vocation of Our Age for Legislation and Jurisprudence.* Translated by Abraham Hayward. London, 1831.

Serov, A.N. *Izbrannye stat'i.* Moscow-Leningrad, 1950.

Speranskii, Mikhail M. "Imperatorskoe Uchilishche Pravovedeniia." *Russkaia Sturina* 12 (1885): i-iv.
    "K L-ti letiu II-go otdeleniia: sobstvennoi E.I.V. Kantseliarii." *Russkaia Starina* 15 : 3 (1876): 586-92.
    "Kratkoe istoricheskoe obozrenie komissii sostavleniia zakonov." *Russkaia Starina* 15 (1876): 433-34.
    Obozrenie glavnykh osnovanii mestnogo upravleniia sibiri (po bumagum Speranskogo i sibirskogo komiteta 1821-1822). St. Petersburg, 1841.
    Obozrenie istoricheskikh svedenii o Svod Zakonov. Sostavlennoe iz aktov kraniashchichsia v II otdelenii Sobstvennoi Ego Imperatorskago Velishestva Kantseliarii. St. Petersburg, 1833.
    "Ob' iasnitel'naia zapiska soderzhaniia i raspolozheniia svoda zakonov grazhdanskikh." *Arkhiv istoricheskikh i prakticheskikh svedenii* 2 (1859): 235-45.
    "O sushchestve svoda." *Russkaia Starina* 15 (1876): 586-92.
    "O svode i sobranii zakonov." *Arkhiv istoricheskikh i prakticheskikh svedenii* 4 (1861): 1-8.

"O zakonakh: Besedy grafa M.M. Speranskogo Ego Imperatorskom Visochesvom Gosudarem Naslednikom Cesarevichem Velikem kniazem Aleksandrom Nikolaevichom s 12-go octiabria 1835 po 20 aprelia 1837 goda." *Sbornik Imperatorskogo Rosskago Istoricheskago Obshchestva* 30 (1881): 331-491.

"O zakonakh rimskikh i razlichii ikh ot zakonov rossiiskikh." *Russkaia Starina* 15 (1876): 592-97.

Plan gosudarstvennago preobrazovaniia grafa M.M. Speranskago. Moscow, 1905.

" 'Propoved' 1791 g." *Russkaia Starina* 109 (February 1902): 283-91.

Precis des Notions historiques sur la formation du Corps des lois russes. St. Petersburg, 1833.

"Predpolozhenniia k okonochatelnomu sostavleniu zakonov." *Russkaia Starina* 15 : 6 (1876): 434-41.

Proekty i zapiski. Edited by S.N. Valk. Moscow and Leningrad, 1961.

Rukovodstvo k poznaniiu zakonov. St. Petersburg, 1845.

Stasov, V.V. "Aleksandr Nikolaevich Serov." *Russkaia Starina* 8 (1875): 581-602.

"Graf Modest Andreevich Korf: Biograficheskii ocherk." *Russkaia Starina* 15 (Jan-Apr 1876): 402-21.

Sobranie Sochinenii. 4 vols. St. Petersburg, 1894-1906.

"Uchilishche Pravovedeniia sorok let toma nazad, 1836-1842." *Russkaia Starina* 12 (1880): 1015-42; 2 (1881): 393-422; 4 (1881): 573-602; 5 (1881): 247-82.

Tiutchev, I.Z. "V Uchilishche Pravovedeniia v 1847-1852 gg: Vospominanii po povodu 50-letnego iubilei Uchilishche." *Russkaia Starina* 48 : 11 (1885): 436-52; 48 : 12 (1885) : 663-78; 49 : 2 (1885): 361-76.

Svod Zakonov Rossiiskoi Imperii. 15 vols. St. Petersburg, 1833.

Books and Dissertations:

Alexander, John. *Catherine the Great: Life and Legend.* New York: Oxford University Press, 1989.

Alston, Patrick A. *Education and the State in Tsarist Russia.* Stanford: Stanford University Press, 1969.

Anisimov, Evgenii. *Empress Elizabeth: Her Reign and Her Russia 1741-1761.* Translated by John T. Alexander. Gulf Breeze, FL: Academic International Press, 1995.
　　　Rossiia v seredenie XVIII veka: Bor'ba za nasledie Petra. Moscow: Mysl', 1986.

Arkhipov, I.V. *Ulozhenie o nakazaniiakh ugolovnikh i ispravitel'nikh 1845g.* Saratov, 1990.

Armstrong, John A. *The European Administrative Elite.* Princeton: Princeton University Press, 1973.

Baranov, P. *Mikhail Andreevich Balug'ianskii 1769-1847.* St. Petersburg, 1882.

Barshev, Ia. *Istoricheskaia zapiska o sodeistvii Vtorogo Otdeleniia sobstvennoi ego I.V. Kantseliarii razviti iuridicheskikh nauk v Rossii.* St. Petersburg, 1876.

Berezkin, S. *Speranskii kak kodifikator.* Odessa, 1889.

Berman, Harold J. *Justice in Russia: An Interpretation of Soviet Law.* Cambridge, MA: Harvard University Press, 1950.

Bervi, V.V. [N. Flerovski]. *Tri Politicheskie sistemy.* Moscow, 1897.

Black, J.L. *Citizens for the Fatherland: Education, Educators and Pedagogical Ideals in Eighteenth Century Russia.* Boulder, CO: East European Monographs, 1979.

Blinov, I. *Gubernatory-istoriko-iuridicheskii ocherk*. St. Petersburg, 1905.

Bushuev, S.K. *A.M. Gorchakov*. Moscow, 1961.

Bychkov, A.F., ed. *V Pamiat' grafa M.M. Speranskogo*. St. Petersburg, 1872.

Byrnes, Robert F. *Pobedonostsev: His Life and Thought*. Bloomington: Indiana University Press, 1968.

Chetvertov, Andrei Mikhailovich. *Pravove polozhenie zapadnikh natsionalnikh raionikh Rossiiskoi imperii v pervoi chetvert XIX v.* Moscow, 1987.

Chibiriav, S.A. *Velikii russkkii reformator: zhizn', deiatelnost' politicheskii vzgliadi M.M. Speranskago*. Moscow, 1993.

Cracraft, James. *The Church Reform of Peter the Great*. Stanford: Stanford University Press, 1971.

Demkov, M.I. *Istoriia russkoi pedagogii*. 2 vols. Revel, 1895.

Dmitriev, Fedor Mikhailovich. *O zaslugakh grafa Speranskago russkom zakonovedenii*. St. Petersburg, 1852.

Dukes, Paul. *Catherine the Great and the Russian Nobility: A Study Based on the Materials of the Legislative Commission of 1767*. Cambridge: Cambridge University Press, 1967.
        Catherine the Great's Instruction (Nakaz) to the Legislative Commission. Newtonville, MA: Oriental Research Partners, 1977.

Fateev, A.N. *Akademicheskaia i gosudarstvennaia deiatelnost' M.A. Balug'ianskago (Balud'ianskago) v Rossii*. Moscow, 1971.
        M.M. Speranskii: Vliianie sredi na sostavitelia Svoda Zakonov v pervii period ego zhizn'. Moscow, 1915.

Flynn, James T. *The University Reform of Alexander I, 1802-1835.* Washington D.C.: Catholic University of America Press, 1988.

Garrard, J.G. ed. *The Eighteenth Century in Russia.* Oxford: Oxford University Press, 1973.

Gleason, Walter. *Moral Idealists, Bureaucracy, and Catherine the Great.* New Brunswick, NJ: Rutgers University Press, 1981.

Golubeva, O.D. *M.A. Korf.* St. Petersburg, 1995.

Got'e, Iurii. *Istoriia oblastnogo upravleniia v Rossii ot Petra I do Ekateriny II.* 2 vols. Moscow, 1913, 1941.

Hans, Nicholas. *History of Russian Educational Policy, 1701-1917.* New York: Russell and Russell, 1964.
   The Russian Tradition in Education. London, 1963.

Hartley, Janet. *Alexander I.* London: Longman, 1994.

Herold, J. Christoper. *The Age of Napoleon.* Boston: Houghton Mifflin, 1963.

Hughes, Lindsey. *Russia in the Age of Peter the Great.* New Haven: Yale University Press, 1998.

Hundley, Helen Sharon. "Speransky and the Buriats: Administrative Reform in Nineteenth Century Russia." Ph.D. dissertation, University of Illinois at Urbana-Champaign, 1985.

Huskey, Eugene. *Russian Lawyers and the Soviet State: The Origins and Development of the Soviet Bar, 1917-1939.* Princeton: Princeton University Press, 1986.

Kaiser, Daniel H. *The Growth of the Law in Medieval Russia.* Princeton: Princeton University Press, 1980.

Kaiser, Friedhelm Berthold. *Die Russische Justizreform von 1864.*
Leiden: E.J. Brill, 1971.

Kelley, Donald R. *Historians and the Law in Postrevolutionary France.*
Princeton: Princeton University Press, 1984.

Kizevetter, A.A. ed. *Istoricheskie ocherki.* Moscow, 1912.

Kliuchevskii, V.O. *Kurs russkoi istorii.* 3 vols. Moscow, 1955-59.
Peter the Great. New York: Vintage, 1961.

Koniuchenko, T. *Statisticheksii svedeniia o lichnom sostave
vospitannikakh i khoziastvennoi chasti, Imperatorskogo Uchilishcha
Pravovedeniia za 50 let ego sushchestvovaniia.* St. Petersburg, 1886.

Korf, M.A. *Zhizn' grafa Speranskago.* 2 vols. St. Petersburg, 1861.

Korkunov, N.M. *Russkoe gosudarstvennoe pravo.* 2 vols. 7th ed. rev.
St. Petersburg, 1909.
            Sbornik statei N.M. Korkunova (1877-1897). St. Petersburg,
1898.

Kornilov, V.A. *Obshchestvenno-politicheskie vzgliadi i deiatel 'nost'
M.M. Speranskago.* Moscow, 1974.

Kosachevskaia, E.M. *Mikhail Andreevich Balug'ianskii i
Petersburgskii Universitet Pervoi Chetvertii XIX veka.* Leningrad,
1971.

Kuprits, N. Ia. *Iz Istorii Gosudarstvenno-pravovoi mysli
dorevolutsnonnoi Rossii (XIXv).* Izdatelstvo: Moskovskogo
Universiteta, 1980.

Latkin, V.N. *Zakonodatel'nye kommissii v Rossii v XVIII st.* St.
Petersburg, 1887.

Leonard, Carol S. *Reform and Regicide: The Reign of Peter III of Russia.* Bloomington, IN: Indiana University Press, 1993.

Lincoln, W. Bruce. *The Conquest of a Continent: Siberia and the Russians.* New York: Random House, 1994.
　　　In the Vanguard of Reform: Russia's Enlightened Bureaucrats, 1825-1861. DeKalb, IL: Northern Illinois University Press, 1982.
　　　Nicholas I: Emperor and Autocrat of All the Russias. DeKalb: Northern Illinois Press, 1989.

Lovel, Colin Rhys. *English Constitutional and Legal History: A Survey.* New York: Oxford University Press, 1962.

Madariaga, Isabel de. *Russia in the Age of Catherine the Great.* New Haven: Yale University Press, 1981.

Maikov, P.M. *O Svode Zakonov Rossiiskoi Imperii.* St. Petersburg, 1905.

Martin, Alexander M. *Romantics, Reformers, Reactionaries: Russian Conservative Thought and Politics in the Reign of Alexander I.* DeKalb, IL: Northern Illinois University Press, 1997.

McConnell, Allen. *Alexander I: Paternalistic Reformer.* New York: Thomas J. Crowell, 1970.

McGrew, Roderick. *Paul I of Russia 1754-1801.* Oxford: Clarendon University Press, 1992.

Minaeva, N.V. *Pravitelstvennii konstitutsionalizm i peredovoe obshchestvennoe mnenie Rossii v nachale XIX veka.* Saratov: Izdatel'stvo Saratovskogo Universiteta, 1982.

Mironenko, S.V. *Samoderzhavie i Reformii Politichskaia Bor'ba v Rossii v nachale XIXv.* Moscow: "Nauka," 1989.

Molchanov, M.M. *Pol-veka nazad: Pervye gody Uchilishche Pravovedeniia v Sankt Peterburg.* St. Petersburg, 1892.

Nechkina, M.V. *Dvizhenie Dekabristov.* 2 vols. Moscow, 1955.

Netting, A.G. "Russian Liberalism: The Years of Promise, 1842-1855." Ph. D. dissertation, Columbia University, 1967.

Nol'de, A.E. *Ocherki istorii kodifikatsii mestnykh grazhdanskikh zakonov pri grafe Speranskom.* 2 vols. St. Petersburg, 1906, 1914.

Olkhovsky, Yuri. *Vladimir Stasov and Russian National Culture.* Ann Arbor, MI: UMI Research Press, 1983.

Orlovsky, Daniel T. *The Limits of Reform: The Ministry of Internal Affairs in Imperial Russia, 1802-1881.* Cambridge, MA: Harvard University Press, 1981.

Osherovich, B.S. *Ocherki po istorii russkoi ugolovno-pravovoi mysli.* Moscow, 1946.

Pakhman, S.V. *Istoriia kodifikatsii grazhdanskogo prava.* 2 vols. St. Petersburg, 1876.

Pashennyi, N. *Imperatorskoe Uchilishche Pravovedeniia i pravovedy v gody miravoiny i smuty.* Madrid, 1967.

Peterson, Claes. *Peter the Great's Administrative and Judicial Reforms: Swedish Antecedents and the Process of Reception.* A.B. Nordiska: Bokhandeln, 1974.

Pipes, Richard. trans. and ed. *Karamzin's Memoir on Ancient and Modern Russia: A Translation and Analysis.* New York: Antheneum, 1966.

Polievktov, M. *Nikolai I: Biografia i obzor tsarstvovaniia.* Moscow, 1918.

Raeff, Marc. *Michael Speransky: Statesman of Imperial Russia, 1772-1839.* The Hague: Martinus Nijhoff, 1957.

    ed. *Plans for Political Reform in Imperial Russia, 1730-1905.* Englewood Cliffs, NJ: Prentice Hall, 1966.

    Political Ideas and Institutions in Imperial Russia. Boulder, CO: Westview Press, 1994.

    The Well-Ordered Police State: Social and Institutional Change Through Law in the Germanies and Russia 1600-1800. New Haven: Yale University Press, 1983.

Riasanovsky, Nicholas V. *A Parting of Ways: Government and the Educated Public in Russia, 1801-1855.* Oxford: Oxford University Press, 1976.

Riasanovsky, V.A. *Mongolskoe pravo – preimuschestvenno obychnoe.* Harbin, 1931.

Richter, Melvin. *The Political Theory of Montesquieu.* Cambridge: Cambridge University Press, 1977.

Romanovich-Slavatinskii, P. *Gosduarstvennaia deiatelnost' grafa Mikhaila Mikhailovicha Speranskago.* Kiev, 1873.

Rozhdestvenskii, S.V. *M.M. Speranskii i komitet 1837 goda o stepeni obucheniia krepost'nikh liudei.* St. Petersburg, n.d.

    Ocherki po istorii sistem narodnago obrazovaniia v Rossii v XVIII-XIX vv. St. Petersburg, 1912.

Saunders, David. *Russia in the Age of Reaction and Reform, 1801-1881.* London: Longman, 1992.

Schil'der, N.K. *Imperator Nikolai Pervyi, ego zhizn' i tsarstvovanie.* 2 vols. St. Petersburg, 1903.

Seleznev, I. *Istorich ocherk Imperatorskogo bivshago Tsarskoselskago nine Aleksandrovskago Litseia.* St. Petersburg, 1861.

Piatidesiatiletnii ubilei Imperatorskogo Uchilishche Pravovedeniia. St. Petersburg, 1886.

Seredonin, S.M. *Graf M.M. Speranskii: Ocherk gosudarstvennoi diatelnosti*. St. Petersburg, 1909.

Shabaeva, M.F. *Ocherki istorii shkoly iz pedagogicheskoi mysli narodov SSSR: XVIII v. – pervaia polovina XIX v.* Moscow, 1973.

Sinel, Allen. *The Classroom and the Chancellery: State Educational Reform in Russia under Count Dmitry Tolstoi*. Cambridge, MA: Harvard University Press, 1973.

Siuzor, Georgii. *Ko dniu LXXV iubileia imperatorskogo uchilishche pravovedeniia 1835-1910*. St. Petersburg, 1910.

Skachkov, I.A. *Kratkii istoricheskii ocherk detskago priuta printsa P.G. Oldenburgskago*. St. Petersburg, 1883, 1896.

Smirnov, F.N. *Obshchestvenno-politicheskie i pravovie vzgliadi A.P. Kunitsyna*. Moscow, 1966.

Smith, Douglas. *Working the Rough Stone: Freemasonry and Society in Eighteenth Century Russia*. DeKalb, IL: Northern Illinois University Press, 1999.

Sobolevskii, V.I. *Imperatorskoe uchilishche pravovedeniia v 1885-1910 godakh*. St. Petersburg, 1910.

Solodkin, I.I. *Ocherki po istorii russkogo ugolovnogo prava*. Leningrad, 1961.

Starr, S. Frederick. *Decentralization and Self-Government in Russia, 1830-1870*. Princeton: Princeton University Press, 1972.

Steinger, C.S. "Government Policy and the University of St. Petersburg,

1819-1849." Ph.D. dissertation, Ohio State University, 1971.

Tel'berg, G.G. *Znachenie "Svoda zakonov" v istorii russkago prava.* Tomsk, 1916.

Thaden, Edward C. *Conservative Nationalism in Nineteenth-Century Russia.* Seattle: University of Washington Press, 1964.

Umanets, F.M. *Aleksandr i Speranskii.* St. Petersburg, 1910.

Uzhakova, S.N. *M.M. Speranskii: Ego zhizn' i obshchestvennaia deiatelnost'.* St. Petersburg, 1891.

Vernadsky, George. ed. *Medieval Russian Laws.* New York: Octagon, 1965.

Von Mohrenschildt, Dimitri. *Toward a United States of Russia: Plans and Projects of Federal Recosntruction of Russia in the Nineteenth Century.* Rutherford, NJ: Associated University Presses, 1981.

Wagner, William G. *Marriage, Property and Law in Late Imperial Russia.* Oxford: Oxford University Press, 1994.

Walicki, Adrzej. *A History of Russian Thought From the Enlightenment to Marxism.* Stanford: Stanford University Press, 1979.
        Legal Philosophies of Russian Liberalism. Notre Dame, IN: University of Notre Dame Press, 1992.

Whittaker, Cynthia. *The Origins of Modern Russian Education: An Intellectual Biography of Count Sergei Uvarov, 1786-1855.* DeKalb, IL: Northern Illinois University Press, 1984.

Wischnitzer, Markus. *Die Universitat Göttingen und die Entwicklung der liberalen Ideen in Russland im ersten Viertel des 19 Jahrhunderts.* Berlin, 1907.

Wortman, Richard. *The Development of a Russian Legal Consciousness.* Chicago: University of Chicago Press, 1976.

Yaney, George. *The Systemization of Russian Government.* Urbana: University of Illinois Press, 1973.

Zaitsev, A.F. *Mirovozzrenie A.P. Kunitsyna (1783-1840 gg).* Moscow, 1951.

Articles, Book Chapters, and Encyclopedia Entries:

Abdurakhmanova, B.M. "Razrabotka M.M. Speranskim ustava o sibirskikh kirgizakh 1822 g. sotsial'no-politicheskie instituty kazakhskogo obshchestva." *Vestnik Moskovskogo Universiteta Seriia 8: Istoriia* 4 (1991): 49-58.

Alekseev, Michael P. "Adam Smith and His Russian Admirers of the Eighteenth Century." In *Adam Smith, As Student and Professor,* ed. William R. Scott, 424-31. New York: Augustus M. Kelley, 1965.

Armstrong, John A. "Old-Regime Administrative Elites: Prelude to Modernization in France, Prussia, and Russia." *International Review of Administrative Sciences* 38 : 1 (1972): 21-40.
 "Tsarist and Soviet Elite Administrators." *Slavic Review* 31 : 2 (1972): 283-90.

Bestuzhev-Riumin, K.N. "Pavel Mikhailovich Stroev." *Russkaia Starina* 15 (Jan-Apr 1876): 426-29.

Black, J.L. "Citizenship Training and Moral Regeneration as teh Mainstays of Russian Schools." *Studies on Voltaire and the Eighteenth Century* 167 (1977): 427-51.

Bogoslovskii, M.M. "Plata ob ulozhenii 1700-1703 gg." *Izvestiia AN SSSR* 15-17 (1927): 1347-1474; 1 (1928): 81-110.

Bokova, V.M. "Tema Zakonnosti v Russkoi pechati nachala XIX v." *Vestnik Moskovskogo Universiteta Seriia 8: Istoriia* 6 (1989): 34-40.

Bouwsma, William. "Lawyers and Early Modern Culture." *American Historical Review* (April 1973): 303-27.

Brown, A.H. "Adam Smith's First Russian Followers." In *Essays on Adam Smith*, eds. Andrew S. Skinner and Thomas Wilson, 247-73. Oxford: Oxford University Press, 1975.

   "The Father of Russian Jurisprudence: The Legal Thought of S.E. Desnitskii." In *Russian Law: Historical and Political Perspectives,* ed. W.E. Butler, 117-41. Leyden: A.N. Sijhoff, 1977.

   "S.E. Desnitsky, Adam Smith, and the Nakaz of Catherine II." *Oxford Slavonic Studies* 7 (1974): 42-59.

Butler, W.E. "F.G. Strube de Piermont and te Origins of Russian Legal History." In *Russia in the Age of the Enlightenment: Essays for Isabel de Madariaga,* eds. Janet Hartley and Roger Bartlett, 125-41. London: Macmillan, 1990.

Bychkov, A.F. ed. "K piatidesiatiletiia II-go otdeleniia sobstvennoi E.I.V. Kantselairii." *Russkaia Starina* 15 (1876): 430-41.

Bychkov, I.A. "K biografii grafa M.M. Speranskago: Materiali zametki barona M.A. Korfa." *Russkaia Starina* 33 (February 1902): 283-306.

Chechulin, N.D. "Ob istochniakakh nakaza." *Zhurnal Ministerstva Narodnago Prosveshcheniia* (April 1902): 306-17.

Christian, David. "The Political Ideals of Michael Speransky." *Slavonic and East European Review* 54 : 2 (April 1976): 192-213.

   "The Political Views of the Unofficial Committee in 1801: Some New Evidence." *Canadian-American Slavic Studies* 12 : 2 (Summer 1978): 247-65.

Chumikov, A. ed. "Speranskii i Balugianskii-uchastie ikh v sostavlenii svoda uzakonenii dlia Pribaltiiskikh gubernii (iz zapisok ochevidtsva: F. Grunval 'dt)." *Russkaia Starina* 35 (July 1882): 41-58.

Cizova, T. "Beccaria in Russia." *Slavonic and East European Review* 40 (1962): 384-408.

Dewey, Horace. "The 1497 *Sudebnik* – Muscovite Russia's First National Law Code." *American Slavic and East European Review* 15 (1956): 325-38.

Dewey, Horace W. and Ann M. Kleimola. "Coercion by Righter (Pravezh) in Old Russian Administration.' Canadian-American Slavis Studies 9:2 (Summer 1975): 156-67

Ditiatina, I. "Ekaterininskaia kommissiia 1767 goda o sochinenii proekta novago ulozheniia." *Iuridicheskii Vestnik* 11:3 (March 1879): 269-302; 11:5 (May 1879): 637-72.

Dmitriev, F.M. "Speranskii i ego gosudarstvennaia deiatelnost'." *Russkii Arkhiv* 6:10 (1868): 1257-1656.

Druzhinin, N.kkP. "Pamiati M.M. Speranskogo." *Istoricheskii Vestnik* 35 (January 1889): 141-64.

Edwards, David W. "Count Joseph Marie de Maistre and Russian Educational Policy, 1803-1828." *Slavic Review* 36:1 (1977):54-75.
    "The System of Nicholas I in Church-State Relations." In *Russiṣan Orthodoxy under the Old Regime.* eds. Robert L. Nichols and Theofanis George Stavrou, 154-69. Minneapolis: University of Minnesota Press, 1978.

Eroshkin, N.P. "Samoderzhavie pervoi polovine XIX veka i ego politicheskie instituti (k voprosu o klassovoi sushchnosti absolutizma)." *Istoriia SSSR* (January-February 1975): 37-59.

Faeteev, A.N. "K istorii i teorii kodifikatsii-stoletie Polnogo Sobraniia Zakonov." *Russkii narodnyi universitet v Prage, Nauchnye trudy* 4 (1931): 3-22.

Federov, V.A. "Arest Dekabristov." *Vestnik Moskovskogo Universiteta Seriia 8: Istoriia* 5 (1985): 59-71.

Filippov, A. "Dva istoriko-iuridicheskikh izdaniia zadumannikh M.M. Speranskim pri Nikolai I." *Istoricheskie Izdaniia* (1916): 26:42.
"K voprosu o sostave pervogo Polnoe Sobranii Zakonov Rossiiskoi Imperii." *Otchet Imperatorskogo Moskovskogo Universiteta za 1915 g.* (Moscow, 1916).
"Speranskii kak kodifikator russkogo prava." *Russkaia Mysl'* 10 (1892): 195-221.
"Znachenie Speranskogo v istorii russkogo zakonodetel'stva." *Russkaia Mysl'* 4 (1889): 1-21.

Flyn, James T. "Russia's University Question': Origins to Great Reforms 1802-1863."*History of Universities* 7 (1988): 1-35.
"s.s. Uvarov's 'Liberal' Years." *Jahrbücher für Geschichte Osteuropas* 20:4 (1972): 481-91.
"The Universities, the Gentry and the Russian Imperial Service 1815-1825." *Canadian Slavic Studies* (Winter 1968): 486-503.

Friedlander, G.M. and M. Dewey. " 'Freiheit und Gezetz' Puskin und die Grosse Frazosische Revolution." *Zeitschrift für slawistik* 34:3 (1989): 329-344.

Gooding, John. "The Decembrists in the Soviet Union."*Soviet Studies* 40:2 (April 1988): 196-209.
"The Liberalism of Michael Speransky." *Slavoșnic and East European Review* 643 (July 1986): 401-24.
"Perestroika as Revolution from within: an interpretation." *Russian Review* 51:1 (1992): 36-57.
"Speransky and kBaten'kov." *Slavonic and East European Review* 66:3 (July 1988): 400-25.

Grot, Ia.K. "Vospominanie o graf M.A. Korf." *Russkaia Starina* 15 (Jan-Apr 1876): 422-25.

Gsovski, Vladimir V. "Medieval Russian Laws: A Review Article." *American Slavic and East European Review* 6 (1947): 152-58.

Hammer, Darrell P. "The Character of the *Russkaia Pravda." Slavic Review* 31:2 (1972): 291-95. "Russia and the Roman Law." *American Slavic and East European Review* 16 (1957): 1-13.

Hartley, Janet M. "Catherine's Conscience Court – An English Equity Court?" In *Russia and the West in the Eighteenth Century,* ed. A.G. cross, 306-18. Newtonville, MA: Oriental Research Partners, 1983.

Hellie, Richard. "Early Modern Russian Law: The Ulozhenie of 1649." *Russian History* 15:2-4 (1988): 155-80.

Hollingsworth, Barry. "A.P. Kunitsyn and the Social Movement in Russia under Alexander I." *Slavonic and East European Review* 43 (1964): 114-29.

Jenkins, Michael. "Mikhail Speransky." *History Today* 20:6 (1970): 404-409.

Jusilla, Osmo. "Finnland in Der Gesetzkodifikation zur Zeit Nikolajs I." *Jahrbücher für Geschichte Osteuropas* 49 : 1 (1972): 24-41.

Kaliagin, V.A. "M.M. Speranski i ego reformy 1808-1812 gg." *Sovetskoe Gosudarstvo i Pravo* 9 (1982): 111-120.

Kaplan, Frederick L. "Tatishchev and Kantemir: Two Eighteenth-Century Exponents of a Bureaucratic Style of Thought." *Jahrbücher für Geschichte Osteuropas* 13 (1965): 503-20.

Kasso, L.A. "K istorii svoda zakonov grazhdanskikh." *Zhurnal Ministervtva Iustitsii* (March 1904): 53-89.

Keep, John L.H. "Justice for the Troops: A Comparative Study of Nicholas I's Russia and France under Louis-Philippe." *Cahiers du monde russe et sovetique* 28 : 1 (1987): 31-54.

Khoch, A.A. "Administrativnaia politika M.M. Speranskogo v sibiri i ustav ob upravlenii inorodtsev' 1822 g." *Vestnik Moskovskogo Universiteta Seriia 8: Istoriia* 5 (1990): 40-49.

Kivelson, Valerie. "The Devil Stole His Mind: The Tsar and the 1648 Moscow Uprising." *American Historical Review* 98 : 3 (June 1993): 733-56.

Kleimola, Ann M. "Law and Social Change in Medieval Russia: The *Zakon sudnyi lyudem* as a Case Study." *Oxford Slavonic Papers* n.s. 9 (1976): 17-27.

Kolumzin, A.N. "Dmitri Nikolaevich Zamiatnin." *Zhurnal Ministerstva Iustitsii* 9 (1914): 233-322.

Korkunov, N.M. "S.E. Desnitskii – pervii russkii professor prava." *Zhurnal Ministers va Iustitsii* 2 (1894): 324-48.

Kosachevskaia, E.M. "A.S. Puskkin i Peterburgskii Universitet." *Vestnik Leningradskogo Universiteta: Seriia Istoriia, Iazyka i Literaturny* 2 (1979): 22-28.
    "Krest'ianskie proekty M.A. Balug'ianskogo." *Istoriia SSSR* 6 (1970): 83-94.

Kucherov, Samuel. "Administration of Justice under Nicholas I of Russia." *American Slavic and East European Review* 7 (1948): 125-38.
    "Indigenous and Foreign Influences on the Early Russian Legal Heritage." *Slavic Review* 31 : 2 (1972): 257-96.

Kuprits, N.Ia. "A.P. Kunitsyn, uchilel' Pushikina, Gosudarstvoved." *Sovetskoe Gosudarstvo i Pravo* 3 (1978): 106-112.

Lang, David M. "Radishchev and the Legislative Commission of Alexander I." *American Slavic and East European Review* 6 (1947): 11-24.

LeDonne, John. "Civilians under Military Justice During the Reign of Nicholas I." *Canadian-American Slavic Studies* 7 : 2 (1973): 171-87.
　　"The Judicial Reform of 1775 in Central Russia." *Jahrbücher für Geschichte Osteuropas* 21 (1973): 29-45.

Levin-Stankevich, Brian L. "The Transfer of Legal Technology and Culture: Law Professionals in Tsarist Russia." In *Russia's Missing Middle Class: The Professions in Russian History.* ed. Harley D. Balzer, 223-50. Armonk, NY: M.E. Sharpe, 1996.

Lincoln, W. Bruce. "The Ministers of Nicholas I: A Brief Inquiry Into Their Backgrounds and Service Careers." *Russian Review* 34 : 3 (July 1975): 308-23.

Lozin-Lozinskii, M.A. "Kodifikatsiia zakonov po russkomu gosudarstvennomu pravu." *Zhurnal Ministerstva Iustitsii* (April 1897): 143-86; (May 1897): 107-73.

Madariaga, Isabel de. "The Foundation of the Russian Educational System by Catherine II." *Slavonic and East European Review* 57 : 3 (July 1979): 369-95.

Maikov, P.M. "Kommissiia sostavleniia zakonov pri imperatorakh Pavle I i Aleksandre I." *Zhurnal Ministerstva Iustitsii* (September 1905): 256-91; (November 1905): 236-82; (December 1905): 189-214.
　　"Speranskii i studenty zakonovedeniia." *Russkii Vestnik* 8 (1899): 609-26; 9 (1899): 239-56; 10 (1899): 674-82.

Makarov, A.N. "K istorii kodifikatsii osnovnykh zakonov." *Zhurnal Ministerstva Iustitsii* 18: 10 (December 1912): 222-78.
　　"Svod Zakonov 1833-1933 zum hundertjahringe Jubiliaum der kodifikation des russischen Rechts." *Zeitschrift für Osteuropaische Geschichte* 7 : 1 (1933): 39-55.

McFarlin, Harold A. "The Extension of the Imperial Russian Civil Service to the Lowest Office Workers: The Creation of the Chancery Clerkship, 1827-1833." *Russian History* 1 (1974): 1-17.
　　"Recruitment Norms for the Russian Civil Service: The Chancery Clerkship in 1833." *Societas: A Review of Social History* (Summer 1973): 61-73.

Medem, M.M. "Moi vospominaniia ob otse moem Mikhaile Andreeviche Balug'ianskom." *Russkii Arkhiv* 3 (1885): 414-32.

Mezhova, K.G. "Ob istochnikakh formirovaniia volnoiubivkh idei dekabristov." *Istoriia SSSR* 5 (1989): 37-46.

Morrison, Kerry. "Catherine II's Legislative Commission: An Administrative Interpretation." *Canadian Slavic Studies* 4 : 3 (Fall 1970): 464-84.

Nemeth, Thomas. "Kant in Russia: The Initial Phase (Cont'd)." *Studies in Soviet Thought* 40 (1990): 293-338.

Nichols, Robert L. "Orthodoxy and Russia's Enlightenment, 1762-1825." In *Russian Orthodoxy Under the Old Regime*. eds. Robert L. Nichols and Theofanis George Stavrou, 67-89. Minneapolis: University of Minnesota Press, 1978.

Nikitin, N.P. "K.I. Arsenev i ego rol v razvitii ekonomicheskoi geografii v Rossii." *Voprosy geografii* 10 (1948): 3-40.

Nol'de, B.E. "Zakony osnovnye v russkom prave." *Pravo* 8 (1913): 447-61; 9 (1913): 524-41.

Papmehl, K.A. "The Problem of Civil Liberties in the Records of the 'Great Commission'." *Slavonic and East European Review* 41 (December 1963): 274-91.

Pintner, Walter. "The Russian Civil Service on the Eve of the Great Reforms." *Journal of Social History* (Spring 1975): 55-68.
"The Social Characteristics of the Early Nineteenth Century Russian Bureaucracy." *Slavic Review* (September 1970): 429-53.

Poliakov, V.L. "O neizvestnoi zapiske M.M. Speranskogo." *Vestnik Leningradskogo Universiteta: Seriia Istoriia, Iazyka i Literatury* 1 (1982): 25-29.

Pontovich, E. "Osnovnye zakony i kodifikatsiia." *Russkaia Mysl'* 7 (1910): 165-90.

Pypin, A.N. "Russkaia otnoshenaia Bentama." *Vestnik Evropy* 4 : 2 (February 1869): 784-819.

Raeff, Marc. "The Bureaucratic Phenomena of Imperial Russia, 1700-1905." *American Historical Review* 84 : 2 (1979): 399-411.

"Codification et droit en Russie imperiale. Quelques remarques comparatives." *Cahiers du monde russe et sovietique* 20 : 1 (1979): 5-13.

"Filling the Gap between Radishchev and the Decembrists." *Slavic Review* 26 : 3 (1967): 395-413.

"Home, School and Service in the Life of the Eighteenth Century Russian Nobleman." *Slavonic and East European Review* 41 (1962): 295-307.

"Le Climat Politique et les Projets de Reforme dans le Premieres Annees du regne d'Alexandre Ier." *Cahiers du monde russe et sovietique* 2 (1961): 415-33.

"L'etat, le gouvernement et la tradition politique en Russie imperiale avant 1861." *Revue d'histoire moderne et contemporaine* 9 (1962): 295-307.

"The Philosophical Views of Count M.M. Speransky." *Slavonic and East European Review* 31 : 77 (June 1953): 437-57.

"The Political Philosophy of Speranskij." *American Slavic and East European Review* 12 : 1 (February 1953): 1-21.

Ransel, David. "Catherine II's Instruction to the Commission on Laws: An Attack on Gentry Liberals?" *Slavonic and East European Review* 50 (1972): 10-28.

Rozhdestvenskii, S. "Soslovniii vopros v russkikh universitetakh v pervoi chetverti XIX veka." *Zhurnal Ministerstva Narodnago Prosveshcheniia* 9 (1907): 83-108.

Sacke, Georg. "M.M. Speranskij i Dekabrysty." *Istoricheskie Zapiski Akademii Nauk SSSR* 102 (1978): 183-222.

Semevskii, V. "Pervii politicheskii traktat Speranskogo." *Russkoe bogatstvo* (January 1907): 46-85.

Seregny, Scott. "The Nedel'shchik: Law and Order in Muscovite Russia." *Canadian-American Slavic Studies* 9 : 2 (Summer 1975): 168-78.

Sergeevich, V.I. "Otkuda geidachi ekateriniskoi zakonodatel'noi kommissii?" *Vestnik Evropy* 13 : 2 (1878): 188-264.

Sinel, Allen A. "Problems in the Periodization of Russian Education: A Tentative Solution." *Slavonic and East European Review* 2 (1977): 54-61.
"The Socialization of the Russian Bureaucratic Elite, 1811-1917: Life at the Tsarskoe Selo Lyceum and the School and Jurisprudence." *Russian History* 3 : 1 (1976): 1-31.

Smirnov, F.N. "Kunitsyn i dekabristy." *Voprosy Istorii* 6 (1967): 216-18.
"Mirovozzrenie A.P. Kunitsyn." *Vestnik Moskovskogo Universiteta* 11 (1966): 88-108.

Taylor, Norman. "Adam Smith's First Russian Disciple." *Slavonic and East European Review* 45 (1967): 425-48.

Tel'berg, G. "Uchastie Imperatora Nikolaia I v kodifikatsionnoi rabote ego tsarstvovanniia." *Zhurnal Ministerstva Iustitsii* (January-March 1916): 233-44.

Thurston, Gary. "P.D. Kiselev and the Development of a Russian Legal Consciousness." *Canadian-American Slavic Studies* 19 : 1 (1985): 1-68.

Walker, Franklin A. "Popular Response to Public Education in the Reign of Tsar Alexander I (1801-1825)." *History of Education Quarterly* 24 : 4 (1984): 527-43.

Whittaker, Cynthia H. "From Promise to Purge: The First Years of St. Petersburg University." *Pedagogica Historica* 18 : 1 (1978): 148-67.

Winavert, M. [Vinaver]. "L'influence francaise sur la codification russe sous Nicolas Ier." *Annales Internationales d'Histoire – Congress de Paris 1900 2e section Histoire comparee des institutions et du droit* (Paris 1902): 155-72.

Wortman, Richard. "Peter the Great and Court Procedure." *Canadian-American Slavic Studies* (Summer 1974): 303-10.

"The Politics of Court Reform." In *Russian and Slavic History,*
eds. Don Karl Rowney and G. Edward Orchard, 10-25. Columbus,
OH: Slavica Publishers, 1977.

Zamuruev, A.S. "Priemy i metody kodifikatsii pri podgotovke proekta
ulozheniia rossiiskogo gosudarstva v 20-e gody XVIII v." In
Vspomopatel'nye istoricheskie distsipliny, eds. M.P. Iroshnikov, et.
al., 117-126. St. Petersburg, 1994.

Zguta, Russell. "The Ordeal by Water (Swimming of Witches) in the
East Slavic World." *Slavic Review* 36 (1977): 220-30.

Reference works:
Clendenning, Philip and Bartlett, Roger., compilers. *Eighteenth Century
Russia: A Select Bibliography of Works Published since 1955.*
Newtonville, MA: Oriental Research Partners, 1981.

Grimsted, Patricia Kennedy. *Archives and Manuscript Repositories
in the USSR. Moscow and Leningrad: Supplement.* Biblioteka Slavica
no. 9 Zug, Switzerland: Int Documentation Co. AG, 1976.
    *Archives and Manuscript Repositories in the USSR. Moscow
and Leningrad.* Studies of the Russian Institute, Columbia University.
Princeton: Princeton University Press, 1972.

Lichnye Arkhivnye Fondy v Gosudarstvennikh khranilishchakh CCCP.
3 vols. Moscow, 1962.

Russkii Biograficheskii Slovar'. 25 vols. St. Petersburg, 1896.

Wieczynski, Joseph L. ed. *Modern Encyclopedia of Russian and Soviet
History.* 58 vols. Gulf Breeze, FL: Academic International Press, 1976-
1992.

Zaionchkovskii, P.A. *Istoriia dorevolutsionnoi Rossii v dnevnikakh i
vospominaniiakh annotirovannyi ukazatel' knig i publikatsii v
zhuranalakh.* 5 vols. Moscow: Izd. Kniga, 1976-1989.

INDEX